FUHR ON GOALTENDING

The problem is that after
you beat Edmonton's defense,
there's Grant Fuhr waiting
for you, and he's the best goalie
in the world for my money.

• • • • • •

Don Cherry

FUHR
ON GOALTENDING

GRANT FUHR   BOB MUMMERY

POLESTAR
BOOK PUBLISHERS

Published and Distributed in Canada by

Polestar Press Ltd., R.R. 1, Winlaw, B.C., V0G 2J0, 604-226-7670

Distributed in the United States by

Slawson Communications Inc., 165 Vallecitos De Oro, San Marcos, CA 92069 619-744-2299

Canadian Cataloguing in Publication Data
Fuhr, Grant, 1962-
Fuhr on goaltending
ISBN 0-919591-28-0
1. Hockey - Goalkeeping.   I. Mummery, Bob, 1947-   II. Title.
GV848.3F84 1988   796.96'227   C88-091576-5

Fuhr On Goaltending was designed by Bob Mummery and Jim Brennan, edited by Stephanie Judy, typeset by Julian Ross, and printed by Gagne Printers.
Printed in Canada

NO TOC

Photo Credits
All photos by Bob Mummery, except for pages 14, 15, 16, 94, and 116.

Acknowledgements
The authors wish to thank the following for their assistance:
Jack Anderson, Victoria Cougars
Banff Holiday Hockey School
Belvedere Cycle & Sport
Gilles Bosse
Mary Brewster, Banff Recreation Director
Daignault-Rolland
Edmonton Oilers
Barry Fraser
Betty Fuhr
Corinne Fuhr
George Guilbault
Mike Loftus
Larry Mitchell, St. Albert Gazette
Gary Mummery
Barry Stafford, Trainer, Edmonton Oilers
Gord Stafford

Grant Fuhr

Grant Fuhr is widely recognized as the world's best hockey goalie. A winner of the Vezina Trophy as the NHL's best goaltender, Fuhr is a perennial all-star who has backstopped the Edmonton Oilers to four Stanley Cup wins in five years. He holds records for most points in a season by a goalie and most games played. In the off-season he is a guest goaltending instructor at summer hockey camps, and an avid golfer.

Bob Mummery

Born in Minnedosa, Manitoba, *Fuhr On Goaltending* is Bob Mummery's third book. His previous books were *The Amazing Oilers*, in 1984, and *Snowbirds: Canada's Ambassadors of the Sky*, in 1985. He is the Official Photographer of the Edmonton Oilers, and has been for the previous eight years. During his career as a professional sports photographer, he has published over four thousand photographs in leading publications, including *Sports Illustrated*, and *Time*. He now resides in Morinville, Alberta with his wife Joyce and two children.

CONTENTS

FOREWARD, BY GRANT FUHR 11

THE FUHR STORY 13

THE BASICS OF GOALTENDING 31

The Fundamentals 32

    Stance and Balance 33

    Skating 34

    Essential Warm-Up 34

    Making Team Practices Work for You 36

Physical Conditioning and Reflex Training 37

    Flip Shot Drill 37

    Nine Puck Drill 38

    Blind Drill 39

    Mirror Drill 40

Stick and Puck Control 41

    Controlling Rebounds 41

    Setting the Puck Drill 42

    Puck Handling 45

    Poke and Sweep Check Drill 46

Body and Positional Saves 50

    Butterfly Save Drill 50

    Split Save 51

    Stacking Pads 52

    Catching the Puck 53

    Defending the Corner Pass Out 54

You've Got to Give Them Something 55

Off-Ice Training 56

    Inner Knee Strengthening 56

    Reflex Drill 1 57

    Reflex Drill 2 58

    Baseball, Table Tennis, and Video Games 59

Twelve Tips 60

GAME ACTION PHOTOS, BY BOB MUMMERY 61

THE GAME 73
Pre-Game Warm-Up 74
Preparing the Crease 75
Temperament 76
Communication 78
The Faceoff 79
Playing the Two on One 80
Playing the Breakaway 81
Playing the Angles 82
Forward Passing 83
Asleep at the Switch 84
The Hook 85
Scouting the Opposition's Goaltender 85

EQUIPMENT 87
Skates 89
Skate Sharpening 90
Goalie Pants 91
Pads 92
Neck Protector 95
Catcher 96
Blocker 97
Mask 98
Goalstick 100
Taping the Stick 102

SCOUTING WITH BARRY FRASER: AN INSIDE LOOK 103
Scouting Grant Fuhr 104
Scouting the Goaltender 106

C.A.H.A. RULES AND REGULATIONS 109

GRANT FUHR: PERSONAL RECORDS 113

Rink Diagrams 117

He's unflappable. He's the
reason they've won four of
the last five Stanley Cups.

• • • • • •

Boston's Gord Kluzak

Foreword
by Grant Fuhr

I have tended the nets for the Edmonton Oilers for eight seasons, during which time we have been fortunate to collect four Stanley Cup rings. During that time my thoughts have often turned to putting something back into the game that I love. Goaltending is a strange and lonely occupation. I hope this book will offer some help and comfort to aspiring goaltenders.

It has been said many times that the goaltender is the forgotten man in minor hockey. Unless you are fortunate enough to have a coach who has played the position, it is a continuous struggle to gather the information and strategy, the positioning, and conditioning that can help make the difference.

One of the breaks that I received was to have Glenn Hall as an assistant coach. I realize that thousands of aspiring goaltenders out there will never have a like opportunity. It is for this reason that I have decided to write this book. I have enjoyed putting this together. If it helps goaltenders play a little better and makes the game more enjoyable for them, then it will have been worthwhile.

THE FUHR STORY

There was never any question in my mind. Goaltending was the only position on a hockey team that I would play. Hockey was my sport and my love of life. Goaltending was the best part of that. The goaltender was different. All the other kids wanted to score goals. I wanted to stop them from doing that. These decisions I made at the grand age of five.

My dad enrolled me in hockey in a part of Edmonton called Kensington. My first game I was crushed when the coach put one of the other kids in the net, so I grudgingly played my first shift on defense. Halfway through the game, our goalie froze his toes (we played on outdoor rinks until I was thirteen) and I was quick to volunteer. From that time to this, goaltending has been my life during the winter months.

Minor Hockey:
From Five to Fifteen

My biggest break during my minor hockey career came when I crossed paths with Glenn Hall, the famous goaltender for the Chicago Blackhawks. One season several of my friends and I had enrolled on a team playing out of our neighboring town of Stony Plain. Glenn Hall was an assistant coach on that team and it was his help and advice that gave me what I needed most at that time. He was somebody to talk to that understood. He was able to point out things that nobody else would notice.

My major advantage was that I had the good fortune to grow up in the small town of Spruce Grove, Alberta. I had lots of ice

time and I was, for the most part, the only goaltender on my team. The amount of game action that I received was a great help. I played against myself, continually working on my game, trying to improve my performance each and every outing.

Don't think I wasn't involved in any bad games. I suffered through my share of blow-outs, too. But no matter what the score happened to be, I found myself hoping the other team would get a breakaway. The challenge of stopping the next shot was what excited me most.

The teams I was fortunate to play on were quite often successful in league playoffs, but rarely were we better than the competition in provincial play. The big city teams were always just too strong. I was never on a championship team until winning the Stanley Cup with the Edmonton Oilers.

I was fourteen when I felt that I might be good enough, that there might be a possibility that I could play for a junior team. The season before, the coach of the Spruce Grove Mets asked me to dress for a couple of games. I spent the games warming the bench and opening the door for the other players, but I had had the taste of junior hockey and I knew that was where I wanted to be.

The next fall I tried out for the St. Albert Saints and played in a couple of games but the coach — Mark Messier's dad! — felt I wasn't quite ready yet and I was cut. It came as a great disappointment because I had dreamed all summer of my chance, and of course always thought I could make it. I was only fifteen at the time, so I knew that there would be other chances. As it was, those other chances came right away. I had

attended a Victoria Cougars development camp which had been held earlier that fall near Spruce Grove. They had expressed some interest in me then, but I knew they had two pretty good goaltenders already who had a couple of years of junior hockey experience, so I felt my chances there were pretty slim. I returned to play midget hockey in Spruce Grove, figuring it would be my turn next year.

It was a pretty exciting day, then, when a letter arrived a few days later from Kenny Larue, a scout for the Victoria team. They were asking my father if he would let me go to Victoria, so that they could have another look at me. After talking to the coach on the phone, my dad drove me out to Victoria. This time I made the team.

At 17 he was the WHL Rookie of the Year. He's the best I've ever seen in junior. There has never been anyone like him.

• • • • • •

Jack Shupe, former coach of the Victoria Cougars, Grant's junior team.

Juniors:
The Victoria Cougars

Once again, as far as goaltending was concerned, I was left on my own to figure out what to do. I learned by watching the other goaltenders, two hundred feet down the ice. I would see the opposing goaltender play a situation a certain way and if he was successful, I would make a mental note of it and use it myself. That's mostly how goaltenders learn, by watching each other.

While I was in Victoria, I rarely thought of playing in the NHL. I had always played hockey to have fun. The game at this level was much faster, but I was still having fun and that was all that mattered. I was playing the game day by day. I was on my own, a thousand miles from home and parents, with all of the distractions that face a young man in that situation. It was a constant struggle to maintain concentration on the game and confidence in myself. The pressure of daily performance was always there, but it bothered me a lot less than it did most of the others on the team. I think in the long run it was my biggest advantage. I was there to have fun and I didn't feel that the rest of my life depended on the game. Fun and enjoyment came first, business second.

I was billeted with a Victoria family, and I worked part-time in a car wash. There wasn't much else that I could do because hockey took most of my time. In the summer I left the game alone. I just worked in the car wash and forgot about hockey. The next time I saw the ice was the first day of training camp that next fall.

My family offered me lots of encouragement during my time in junior hockey. They also kept reminding me that education should play a large part in my life at that time, that an NHL career was not guaranteed. By this time, though, I had decided that it was the NHL or bust.

Scouts:
The NHL
is Watching

Wayne Gretzky with Grant at the NHL Draft.

While I was in juniors, I was never aware of when I, personally, was being scouted. During the games, we'd see the scouts huddled up in the corner of the building, looking a little out of place, but we had a good club in Victoria, and they could be there looking at any one of fifteen players. When the scouts were there, we all played our hardest.

After a game, the scouts never approached anyone, and we were never told which NHL teams might be interested in us. Of course the rumor mills in the dressing room were always at work, but no one was ever quite sure.

It was the agents that came to us. Constantly. They were around more than the coaches were. I found it best to refer them back to my father. He was in a much better position to discuss the possibilities with them than I was. My concentration had to be on the games at hand.

When the time for the NHL draft came around, I didn't care where I went, just as long as I got drafted. The rumor mill had me going to New York. Right up to the time when my name was called by the Oilers, I was sure I was going to the Rangers.

The year before I was drafted, I spent some time in the rink in Edmonton where the Oilers were having their training camp. I was there just to watch, and I didn't talk to anyone. I had not had one conversation with anyone in the Oilers organization, and that is why it was such a shock to me when I was drafted by them in the first round. I was very happy that they did draft me. Playing in your home town has drawbacks—there is no doubt about that, it would have been easier to play somewhere else—but I wanted to play here. I knew Edmonton. I didn't have to adjust to a new life style.

Off to the Oilers

At first training camp

My agent at that time was pretty confident that I would be drafted somewhere in the first round. He paid for my flight down to Montreal and my expenses while I was there for the draft. After the draft was over he let us loose on Crescent Street. It was my first experience in the big big city.

I met some of the Oilers at some functions that summer, but I really didn't have much to do with management or the coaches until I got to camp. I went to my first Oiler training camp as an underage. I still had a year of junior left, so I went there with the idea that I would try my best. If I didn't make the team right away, I would go back to junior, work hard that season and make the team at the training camp next year.

As it was I had a shaky start. One thing in my favor was that Victoria had the same kind of hockey club as the Oilers — the run and gun offense. I was all too familiar with that style of play. The one difference was that here, on the ice, were all the guys I had watched on TV. It was definitely a shaky feeling. There were three of us trying for the two goaltending jobs — Andy Moog, Ron Low, and myself. There wasn't really any indication, as far as I was concerned, about my future until

they sent Andy Moog down to the farm team in Wichita. That left Ron Low and me, and I knew I had made the team.

It was the pace, the incredible speed of the game, that struck me the most. It was about three times quicker in the NHL than it was in junior. The quickness of the shots took me by surprise. Some of the kids in junior shot just as hard as those in the NHL, but in Edmonton they got the shot off at amazing speed. Shooting in stride is a difficult part of the game to develop, but it seemed up here they all were doing it. It was no longer the puck carrier standing there with his head down, signalling that a shot was coming.

Grant with Ron Low

I soon found that up here they would be looking as they shot instead of having their head buried. You couldn't cheat. The quickness of the shot is the NHL goaltender's constant nightmare. Shooting while in stride — that is what took me the longest time to adjust to.

Goaltending in the NHL

I've never seen a goalkeeper

his age with so much

composure. He just stands

there making save after save.

• • • • • •

Wayne Gretzky, commenting
on Fuhr during the first year
of Grant's career.

My first league game in the NHL was against the Winnipeg Jets. We lost the game by a score of 3 to 1, two of which I let in and the third was into an empty net. Strangely, it didn't bother me at all.

My teammates were very supportive, especially Ron Low. It must have helped, because I went back out and didn't lose another one for twenty-three games straight.

19

In the first year of my career, Glen Sather put Ron Low and myself together as room-mates. It was the best thing that happened to me. Ron had good work habits, and just by watching him I picked up the same habits. As far as helping me technically, his advice was, ''Don't try to play my style. Develop and play your own.'' In other words, use what you feel is best for you and not what you see someone else doing. If you feel that the split save is quicker than stacking pads, use it. Keeping the puck out is what counts. It doesn't matter how you go about it. I have to credit Ron Low with helping me the most during my career.

It was January before I lost another game—heady stuff. We finished off the season pretty well and then in the first round of the playoffs I experienced the biggest shock of my life. We got blown out big-time in the Los Angeles series. That whole playoff series was not a happy situation. I didn't play well—too much thought, not enough play. I tried to think everything through instead of just playing. During the games I found myself trying to outthink the opposition instead of out-playing them. Los Angeles knocked us out of the playoffs in the fifth game.

We finished hockey that year in early April. We all learned a few things from that experience.

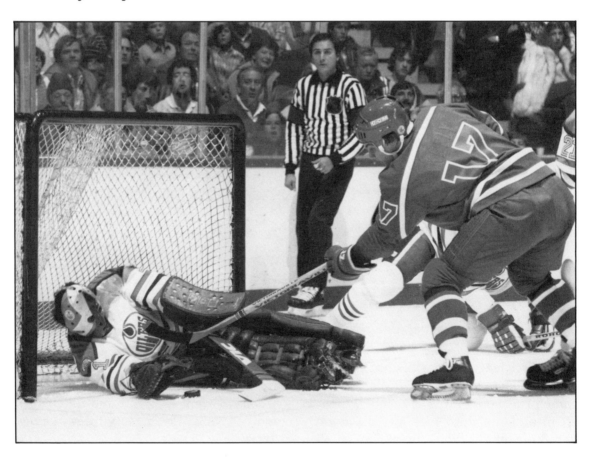

That summer I had an operation on my shoulder. There was a pin inserted in it and the recuperation process was slow. I spent eight weeks with my arm in a sling and I wasn't able to do much except eat. I was a little heavy when I got to camp, and I wasn't sure if my arm would work or not. As a result I got a late start. I lost my confidence and I never really did get off the ground. It wasn't long before I found myself playing hockey in Moncton—a quick taste of reality, and a good move on Glen Sather's part. After playing ten straight games in fourteen nights, I got back into shape in a hurry, both physically and mentally. It certainly opened my eyes.

I returned to Edmonton in a new frame of mind. You can't let your mind wander and worry about your teammates or any-body or anything else. If you don't have confidence in yourself, you cannot play goal. You must have your mind on your game. You must know that you can play. It makes a big difference.

A goaltender must be in as good a shape as every other player on the team. A goaltender who plays a lot can be three or four pounds heavy, but it is imperative that you are as ready as everybody else.

As it turned out, it just wasn't going to be my year. We did get to the Stanley Cup finals, but I found myself watching all four final games. Andy Moog was playing well and it was my turn to watch. Even so, it was a great experience just being in the finals, even if I was watching from the bench. I got to see what the Stanley Cup finals were all about.

Y*ou can't doubt yourself.*

If you doubt yourself, you

will lose.

● ● ● ● ●

Grant Fuhr

My First All-Star Game

One of the biggest thrills of my life was being chosen for the All Star team in my rookie year with the Oilers. The game was played in Washington, and the main event was a luncheon at the White House. I couldn't help but wonder. In seven months I had come from the Victoria Cougars to the NHL All Stars.

The All Star game is for fun. It's basically a chance for the forwards to put on an offensive show. My worry was being embarrassed. Here were the best scorers in the league, all gunning for the most goals, and I was the one on the spot. Just that thought alone made me play my best. That doesn't mean that All Star goaltenders don't have as much fun as everybody else. It's just a little harder on them. During my second year, I wasn't chosen to play in the All Star game, but I have been chosen to play in every one since.

Paul Coffey, Wayne Gretzky, Grant Fuhr, and Mark Messier.

My First Drink From the Cup

The end of the 1983-84 season found our team in a strong position in the league, and as we got closer to the final round, I found that the jitters weren't quite as bad as the first time. We were playing the New York Islanders for the second year in a row. We won the first game on the Island and lost the second one there, and then we returned home for games three, four and five. We won games three and four, but in game four I got hit and my shoulder went out again. I was finished for the series. Andy Moog came in and we won the fifth game and the Stanley Cup. That is the greatest feeling of my life. The first Stanley Cup. I watched the final game on television in the Oilers dressing room. I wasn't disappointed that my injury had happened. Winning the Cup took care of all that.

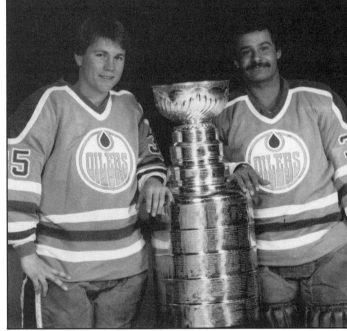

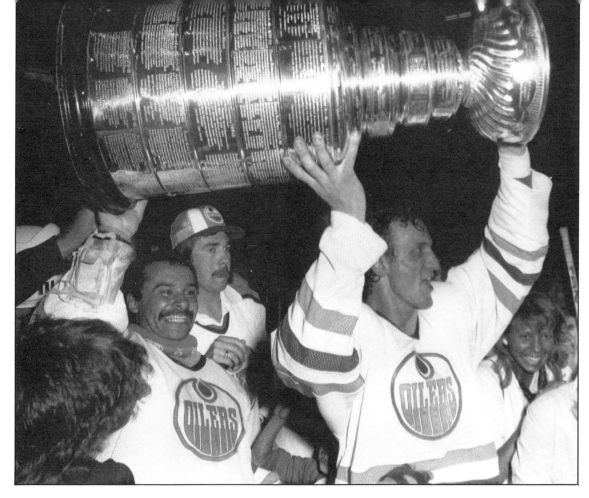

NHL Greats

Kent Nillson

Paul Coffey

Mario Lemieux

The greatest player that I've played against thus far in my career is Mario Lemieux, with Kent Nilsson running a close second. Kent Nilsson had natural raw talent. Maybe even as much talent as Gretzky. Unfortunately he just never seemed to have quite the same desire as Gretzky. But then, I don't think I have ever played against a person who did have as much desire as Wayne.

Mario has unbelievable talent, and since the '87 Canada Cup, he's developed the desire, too. That in itself makes him scary to face. Lemieux is a smart hockey player, very good with the puck, and he seems to know where everybody is on the ice. The only other player I have ever seen that had that sense of awareness was Gretzky. As well, Mario is a great passer. He seems to find the open guy all the time, so that is what you look for. Hopefully the way we will work it against those two is that I will take either Wayne or Mario, and my defenseman will take the open guy. If you don't do that, they will both kill you with their playmaking abilities. Playing against either of those two, you must be aware at all times of where the open man is going.

As far as great point men, names like Coffey and Bourque immediately come to mind. Both have low hard shots and they always go to your stick side. Even knowing that, and I am sure every goaltender in the NHL knows that, either player is still capable of scoring forty or forty-five goals in a season. A low and hard shot is a defenseman's greatest asset. Firstly, a low shot is easily deflected by a teammate, and secondly, the low shot has less chance of being blocked by the legs or upper body of opposing players. Also, the low shot is much harder for the goaltender to see when it comes in through traffic in front of the net.

If you were to ask me which player in the NHL would have my number so to speak, the answer would surprise you. It would have to be Tony McKegney. Every time we play against him, he seems to get a point or two on me. There's no explaining it, but over the years, in my mind at least, he has my number.

Brian Hextall

Billy Smith

Tony Esposito

Ranking very close to Tretiak on my list of all time great goaltenders would be Glenn Hall, Tony Esposito, and Gump Worsley.

More recently, Billy Smith would have to rank as one of my favorites along with Gerry Cheevers and quite possibly, in the near future, Ron Hextall. Hextall's greatest weakness is his emotions, but with time that will cure itself, and when it does, look out. He has all the moves and may be the fastest goaltender I have ever seen.

Soviet Stars

It is one of the disappointments of my career that I never did get an opportunity to play against Vladislav Tretiak. I would have during the 1984 Canada Cup, but I came up with a knee injury and was scratched from that series. Unfortunately, that was his last Canada Cup and consequently my last chance to play against him.

However, over the years I've had several opportunities to watch him play. He was a big man and seemed to know where the puck was going—he was almost always there before the puck. I guess in the final analysis that defines a great goaltender. With his unbelievable quickness, raw speed, and perfect balance, I have to say that he was the greatest goaltender of all time.

Alexander Yakushev was probably the greatest Russian forward that I played against. He was so fast with the puck, that just watching him cross the blue line, you knew you were in trouble. Of late though, the Russians have been unable to replace Tretiak, and so they don't dominate us like they used to. Milnikov is a good goaltender. He has played very well against me in the past and I would have to say he is their best prospect, but again, he is not Tretiak. Their forwards are starting to age a little and the younger players haven't seemed to gel together as well as the old teams.

One On One
With Ninety-Nine

With the recent trade between the Oilers and Los Angeles, I'm going to find out what all of the other NHL goaltenders already know. I'm going to go one on one with Gretzky. I haven't spent a lot of time thinking about it yet, but I'm sure as the time approaches for the first meeting between the Oilers and the Kings, thoughts of Gretzky will cross my mind.

He is the greatest player of all time. In my mind there is just no doubt about it. Our first meeting will certainly not be our *first* meeting. Over the last eight years I've taken thousands of shots from Gretzky in practice. In fact, Andy Moog and I may be the most experienced goaltenders in the world as far as Gretzky is concerned. But that's in practice. The game is an entirely different matter.

Wayne is an extraordinarily smart hockey player. He waits until you make a mistake and then he capitalizes on it. Gretzky has played so long in the league now that everyone knows how he plays. In certain situations he will do one of two or three things. It's not that there is any great secret. The problem is stopping him. He always leaves himself an option to either shoot or pass. However, when we play against each other, we'll each have a 50/50 chance to win. I'm looking forward to facing him.

THE BASICS
OF GOALTENDING

The Fundamentals

If I were to send my son out to play goal for the very first time, my advice would be to have fun. Have fun. Don't worry about fundamentals or anything like that. If goaltending is meant for you, the technique will develop mostly by itself. Up to the age of ten or so, play for the pure enjoyment of the position.

I am very much in favor of the idea that up to that age everyone on the team should have an opportunity to play every position. It's difficult to understand the problems encountered at each position unless you experience them first-hand. You will find fewer goaltenders criticizing their defensemen and vice-versa if they've each experienced each other's situations.

If you've decided that goal is your position, you'll need one important physical trait: *You must not be afraid of the puck*. It isn't a matter of courage, but of reflex. In other words, it's not a mental attitude, but an innate physical ability. Some people will always flinch when an object is hurled at them, and others, knowing that they are protected against it, will not. Even when you're in the stands, behind the plexiglass that you know isn't going to break, do you flinch when the puck is shot straight at you? The vast majority of people do. Being successful in goal means that this most natural reaction must be totally under your control.

Make no mistake about it—equipment today is very safe and protective, but a frozen puck shot at 100 miles an hour will still be felt, and sometimes very much so. If you're afraid of the puck, then you must switch to another position.

I am constantly amazed each summer, when I appear at hockey schools, at the number of kids playing goal who are afraid of the puck. A goaltender can't duck or move aside. Even a mere blink can make the difference between stopping the puck or not. When you step into the net, your job is to stay there and stop the puck at all costs.

By the age of nine or ten, you'll know if goaltending is for you or not. You'll have a feeling for the position. You're ready to start specialized training. Give yourself time to develop. At this early age, counting goals against is ridiculous. If you enjoy playing the position, no matter how good or bad you feel you are, it is time to start on the fundamentals.

Stance and Balance

The basic stance of the goaltender, used throughout most of the game, must be comfortable. A good stance means good balance and readiness to react:

• Legs slightly apart, knees bent slightly
• Weight on the flat part of the blades, slightly towards the front
• Weight even on both skates
• Chest and shoulders slightly forward of the center of gravity

If your balance is too far forward or back—in other words, if your weight is on the toes or heels of your skates—you will react too slowly if a quick sideways or backwards movement is required.

Hold your glove hand at your side with the pocket area facing outwards, and keep your stick hand all the way down the shaft and resting on the shoulder or paddle of the stick. Maintain slight pressure on the stick, keeping the blade flat on the ice and a couple of inches ahead of your skate blades. Keeping the stick just slightly out in front of your skates is a good habit as this will allow the stick to reflex when a puck hits it and cushions the shot, making it easier to handle.

I have found that leaning on the stick, using just enough pressure to keep my weight on the flat part of my skate blades, is also just the right pressure to keep the stick firmly planted on the ice. Even on a side to side motion across the crease, pressure on the blade of the stick is a must.

Balance is the single most important aspect of goaltending. Stay on your feet, and when you fall down, be able to get back up without being awkward. You have to return to the ready position at great speed. You hear a lot of talk about the goalie who flops or goes down too much. All goaltenders must go to the ice many times during a game. The problem is not "going down"—it is returning to your feet too slowly. The quick recovery can only be practiced one way—by doing it. Summer and winter, practicing a quick recovery while retaining balance will benefit your overall performance.

Skating

You often hear hockey people say that the goaltender should be the best skater on a team. This just isn't true—in fact, this kind of thinking can be dangerous. Why should a goaltender, wearing up to fifty pounds more equipment, be asked to compete with the skaters for fifteen to twenty minutes of grueling skating drills, and then go immediately between the pipes in an exhausted condition? This can only increase the possibility of him suffering a serious injury because of a lessened reaction time.

Certainly a goaltender has to be a good skater, and should take part in general skating drills, but agility, balance, and lightning-fast reflexes are far more important than raw speed. The goaltender's job is to react fast—not to skate fast.

Essential Warm-Up

Before you take part in any activity on-ice, either a practice or a game, you do nothing—NOTHING!—until you've done your basic stretching exercises. It takes only one "cold" split save to pull a groin or tear a knee ligament, and you're out of action for months.

The basic idea is to use all the muscles that you'd use during a game, through their full range of movement, but at a much slower pace, slowly working up to game rhythm. Note that goalies need a lot more lower-body exercise than other players in order to protect the areas where almost all injuries to goalies occur—the groin and the knee.

When you first step onto the ice, take a light skate for two or three minutes. Then, find an out-of-the-way spot, often right in front of your bench, to perform some leg stretching exercises (photo above) and then some abdominal stretching exercises as shown in the photo at the left. Go easy at first, only doing these stretches about half-way, and slowly working up to completion.

Making Team Practices Work for You

A normal minor hockey practice does not involve a large amount of instruction aimed specifically at the goaltender. It is virtually impossible to spend that kind of time on one position when there are breakouts and power plays and penalty killing and skating drills to be done which involve the whole team. You can't blame the coach. It is simply that he must instruct the team on drills that involve the most players. There are things that you can do, however, on your own, that will go a long way to developing your own skills.

During those hundreds of three on twos and various other line rush drills, work on your fundamentals. Always be thinking ahead. Remember to stay square to the puck—your shoulders and your pads facing straight at the puck, wherever it may be. Try different things, concentrating on the techniques you're weakest at. When a shooter comes in close enough, try a poke check. When the shooter cuts across the front of your crease, use a split save. Alternate this from one side to the other and then do the stacked pads save, again towards both sides of the net. Determine which of the two basic close-in saves you are more adept at. That's the one to use in game situations.

Few effective drills for the goaltender can be done by yourself. Most drills involve at least one other player. You should always be able to find ten or fifteen minutes during each practice to do some of the following drills:

- Flipshot drill
- Nine puck drill
- Blind drill
- Mirror drill
- Setting the puck drill
- Poke check and sweep check drill
- Butterfly drill

Remember that doing a drill once and then forgetting it is not the answer. It is constant repetition that burns the fundamentals into your mind and allows you to perform them in a split second during game conditions.

Physical Conditioning & Reflex Training

Flip Shot Drill

A drill that I have always liked requires just one of your teammates with a pile of pucks, standing at the top of the slot. This drill allows the goaltender to develop a feel for the puck.

Have your teammate flip the pucks at you, varying the height and speed of the flip shots. Just float the pucks in, one at a time, aiming all over the net. At younger ages when puck control hasn't become a common thing with your teammates, have someone throw the pucks at you. This insures that most of the pucks will be on the net. Fielding hundreds of pucks off your pads, catcher glove, and blocker in this manner helps develop your hand and eye co-ordination.

Nine Puck Drill

Here's a drill that lets you work on three skills at once:

—improve your forward skating while keeping square to the puck

—increase your speed getting up off the ice and regaining your stance

—practice leaving the crease to cut down the angle of the shooter and scrambling back into the crease at the ready position.

Set up three sets of three pucks placed around the crease about five feet out as shown in the diagram. With a teammate standing behind the pucks, the goaltender starts in his crease at the ready position. The goalie skates out to where he can reach the pucks with his stick and pushes the first puck to the shooter. The goaltender drops to his pads in a butterfly position and then regains his stance and blocks the shot. He then skates backwards to the crease and repeats the process again until all nine pucks have been shot.

This is one of my favorite drills and also one of the most grueling.

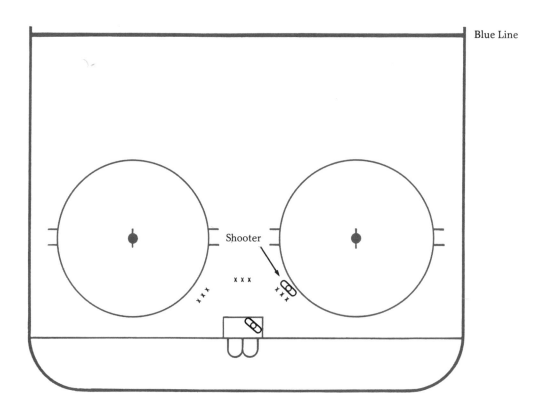

Blue Line

Shooter

Blind Drill

All too often the goaltender's only part in a practice is to face his entire team standing at the blue line firing pucks at him, one after another, and from one side to another. The following drill adds a little excitement to this type of target practice.

The goaltender stands in his crease and faces backwards, looking to the net. Three teammates spread out across the ice, each with a puck. One at a time and in no particular order, each teammate will slap his stick on the ice and immediately shoot the puck at the net. It is the goaltender's function to listen for the sound of the slap, judge which team-mate it came from, and turn to face and stop the shot.

You have to be quick and you have to concentrate, but with this drill, you will learn to do both very quickly. Many times after practice, Marty McSorley and I used to stay out on the ice a few minutes longer than the others just to practice this drill. Remember to not get frustrated at the beginning. It does take a little practice to become adept at this drill, but I think the rewards are great. It will improve your performance in both reaction time and concentration during game situations.

Keep reminding your teammates that this can be a dangerous drill. Make sure that they realize this and they keep their shots below the chest area.

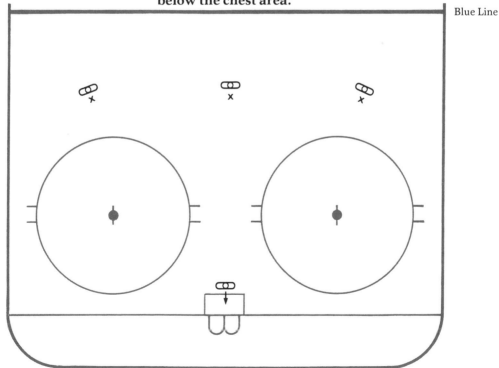

Blue Line

Mirror Drill

The mirror drill is performed using two goaltenders. Both goaltenders square off facing each other and one of the goaltenders being the leader first makes a save movement such as the split save, and the other goaltender facing him must duplicate that movement almost instantaneously. Such movements as the butterfly, stacking pads, forwards and backwards skating, dropping to the knees, extending either the catching glove or blocker, etc., can be used. After one goaltender has led for a few minutes, then the other goaltender should take over and the roles are reversed. You should try to find some time for this drill, even if it is only five or ten minutes every two or three practices.

It is competitive drills like this one that enhance your co-ordination skills and reaction time and drives you to excel, by not being outdone by your teammate.

STICK AND PUCK CONTROL

Stick and Puck Control

Controlling Rebounds

It is commonly said that the first shot on net is the job of the goaltender to stop, the second shot is the responsibility of the defensemen. On many occasions the goaltender can be down on the ice and out of position and not be able to get a good angle on the second shot. It is therefore a must that if it is impossible to gain control of the puck after the save, you must be able to control the direction of the rebound, taking it out of harms way.

Once again, if you are alert during drills and team practices, you will find many opportunities to perfect your technique. Here are the three basic types of rebound control:

1) On medium low shots, flexing the pads downwards will drop the puck into your feet where you can either smother it or where you or a defenseman will be able to gain control and clear it safely out of your zone.

2) When the puck is coming in too hard, and knocking it downwards is unsafe, then it must be steered into the closest corner. Angling your pads slightly toward the nearest corner will deflect the puck in that direction. This can also be done with your blocker hand or your chest protector. I try not to deflect the puck to the corner unless I have no other choice. I have always preferred to knock the puck down in front of me and then control where the puck will go with my stick.

3) Rebounds off the goalstick can be dampened somewhat by holding your stick slightly in front of your skates. This allows some cushioning of the speed of the puck.

Setting the Puck

This drill will improve your skills at retrieving the puck when it is dumped into your zone and setting it up for your defenseman. Have a teammate stand at both points and alternate hard shots around the net. Here are the important things to remember, both in a drill and, more importantly, in a game:

1) Always leave the net on the same side as the puck is coming in from.

2) Get to the boards behind your net before the puck gets there. This is of utmost importance in this situation. Once the goalie commits himself, he is in no-man's land if he misses it.

3) Stop the puck with your stick if you can. Sometimes it is possible only by using your body against the boards. It is obvious that once you have committed yourself to going behind the net, you must gain control of the puck or you will be completely out of position.

4) Once you have gained control of the puck, set it up for your defenseman. The best place to spot or place the puck for easy pickup by your defenseman is on the goal line, approximately three to four feet off to his side of your net. Doing this will allow your defenseman two options. He may either carry the puck past the

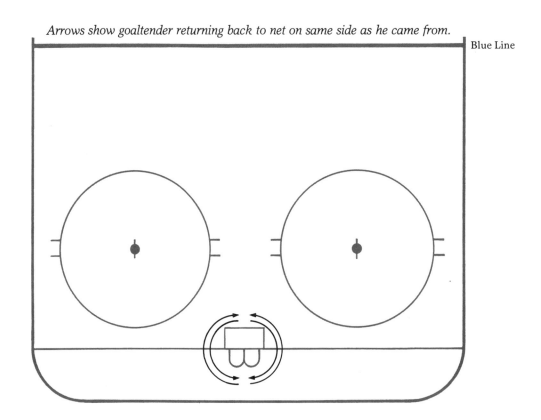

Arrows show goaltender returning back to net on same side as he came from.

Blue Line

front of your net, or behind the net. Avoid spotting the puck directly behind your net, as your defenseman could be cut off or trapped by an opposing forward.

5) Whenever possible, after going to the boards to set up the puck, return to your net from the same direction that you left it. This means leaving the net, stopping, spotting the puck and returning to the net on the same side.

Remember here that you always have the option of not spotting the puck, but instead shooting the puck to a returning forward. This is often used when your defenseman is being too closely covered. This play by the goaltender is relatively new to the game and it has had some

spectacular results. During practice is the time to make your forwards aware and ready to expect this clearing pass. It is a play that the Oilers have perfected over the years. It generally results in one or two of the opponents being trapped well behind the puck and many games have been won on just this sort of play.

You should try to spend at least five minutes every practice on this drill. The ability to stop the puck behind the net is a skill the NHL scouts look for. Barry Fraser, the Oiler's chief scout, always says that having a goalie who's quick behind the net means having a sixth man on your side.

X indicates the spot where the puck should be set for your defensemen.

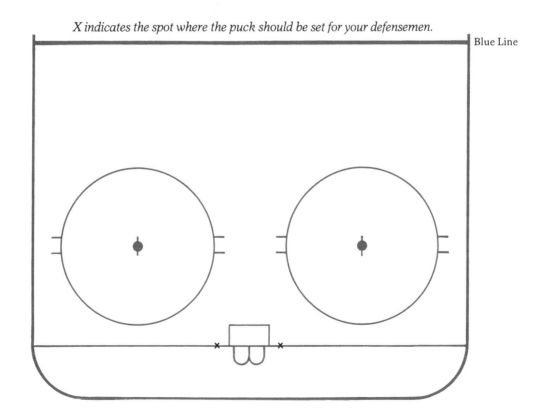

Blue Line

Stopping the puck behind the net.

Puck Handling

Nothing can turn a game around faster than using the goaltender as part of the offense. Clearing the puck to a waiting forward just inside the red line has led many games to a quick end.

You must learn early to shoot the puck without reversing your hands on the shaft of your goalstick. It is a most awkward thing to do, but the dividends will be many. If it is necessary for you to switch hands on the shaft before taking the shot, then you must also use a flat bladed stick, which reduces the amount of snap or speed in your shot. Also, the time lost in making this movement will often be the difference between being successful and being beaten.

It is important to start developing puck control at an early age. Spend a few minutes in every practice on your wrist shot and flip shot. You can practice these off-ice, too. But *always* remember to shoot without reversing your hands on the stick. Forearm and wrist strength are essential for quick, hard, and accurate shots.

The goalstick is much heavier and less flexible than a regular stick and good arm strength is needed to bend or flex the stick on the wrist shot. Any wrist strengthening exercises will ultimately increase the power of your shot.

The game has developed to the stage where the goalie must fire the puck up to the powerplay forwards at the red line in order to cut the ice in half. This develops the speed of the power play attack, since the forwards or defense don't have to constantly skate back behind their own net to retrieve the puck. A goaltender who is able to clear the puck out of danger when the team is shorthanded is also a very valuable commodity.

Poke & Sweep Check Drill

The poke check is one of the more important defensive weapons in a goaltender's arsenal. Most of the line rushes you will experience will have one of the forwards carrying the puck to the net from either side rather than from directly in front from the slot. If your defenseman is covering the forward without the puck, a pass is impossible. Therefore the forward carrying the puck is left with the option of either shooting from a bad angle or crossing in front of the net, close to the goaltender. The moment for the poke check comes when the forward is within the distance that can be covered by the entire length of your body with your arm extended plus the length of your goalstick. You will be amazed to find that this distance can be as much as twelve to fourteen feet.

The poke check is performed by flinging your entire body forward flat on the ice and at the same time pushing your stick at the puck. It is necessary that you totally commit yourself to this move if you are to be successful. You need to surprise the forward, so there can be no halfway measure. It is necessary that you practice this drill often or it will not come across with full effect in game action. *(Photos on following pages.)*

To set up the drill, place the pucks as in the diagram—one puck at each faceoff

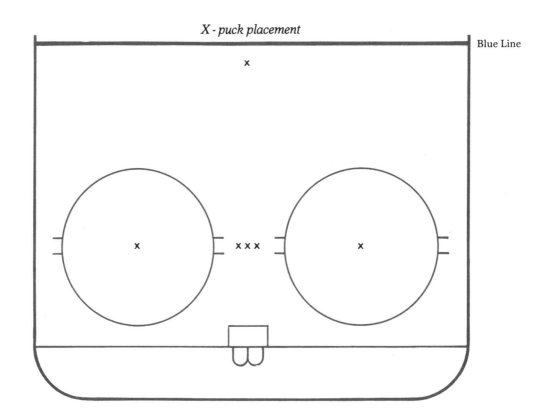

X - puck placement

Blue Line

dot, one in the slot just inside the blue line, and three in the slot at the hashmarks. You will need help from one of your teammates or coaches.

1) Your first move is to the puck just inside the faceoff dot to your right. Approximately two fast strides should bring you within range of this puck. Drop flat to the ice, with your stick, arm, and body fully extended. With both hands high on the shaft of the stick, hook the puck hard to the corner — a sweep check.

2) Hit or miss, get back up to your feet immediately, into the top of your crease and take three shots from a teammate with the three pucks placed in the slot at the hashmarks.

3) As soon as the third puck is shot, immediately move to the other puck at the faceoff dot to your left and sweep

that puck to the left corner.

4) Return to the net and assume the stance. The forward will then have collected the puck at the blue line and, choosing whichever faceoff circle he wishes, he will carry the puck around either of the faceoff dots and across the net, at which time you will attempt the poke check.

If you do not have a teammate to help with this drill, you can still practice by yourself. Place pucks out in front of your net at varying distances and poke check each one, one at a time, until you are confident in the move. The drill described above is a grueling one, but keep in mind that a drill that doesn't make you work hard doesn't do you or your physical condition any good.

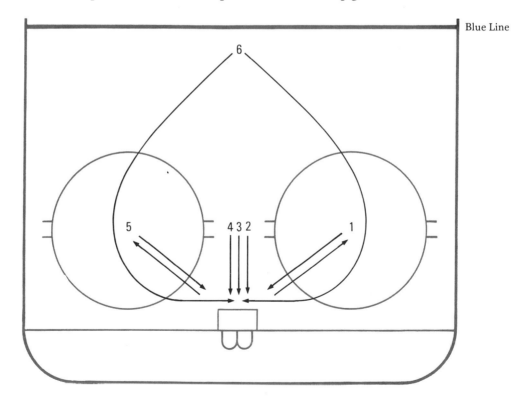

Blue Line

47

Sweep Check

Poke Check

Poke Check Drill

I *don't know where he finds the energy. He just works hard game in and game out. The more he plays, the better he gets.*

• • • • • •

Teammate Steve Smith

Body and Positional Saves

Butterfly Save

This is the type of save I use the most. Perhaps seventy percent of my "going down" saves will be the butterfly. I have found that reflex time in getting back up to your feet from this position is the quickest. It also lets you keep control of your stick, as well as keeping your glove hand near the ice surface in order to smother the puck in the event of a rebound.

The butterfly is performed by dropping to your knees with the sides of your pads laying flat on the ice, pointed to each goalpost. Your pads should be in a "V" shape. Keep in mind that it is most important that your stick remain firmly on the ice and in between your pads.

The drill that I use for this save is simple:

• Count the number of times you can drop to a butterfly save and regain a full balanced stance in a 10-second period. Learn to regain your full stance without using either of your arms or your stick to push yourself back to your feet.

With practice, you should be able to drop and regain your stance ten times, once per second.

Split Save

The split save, in all its variations—the skate save, toe save, and pad save—is useful when the puck is coming in low and to the outside. Always extend the leg that's nearest the path of the puck. Drop to one knee and extend the other leg to meet the path of the puck.

- If the puck is low to the ice, your skate blade must be flat, in full contact with the ice, and turned at an angle that will deflect the puck into the corner and not back into the net.

- If the puck is off the ice, then your toe is extended upwards, leaving only the heel of the skate in contact with the ice.

The guy's a machine.

I can't believe the way

he plays every night.

• • • • • •

Teammate Craig MacTavish

Stacking Pads

This is perhaps the most difficult movement that you will have to master. You will use the stacking pads save when a pass is made from one side of your crease to the other. If the pass is made far enough out from you, and you are unable to deflect or smother the puck, then pads first across the crease is the quickest and most effective defense. Your other option, and the most natural one, is to dive head first with glove extended over to the far post. However, your glove, no matter how big it is, does not present anywhere near as large a blocking area as both your pads, one stacked upon the other. In the picture showing this move, you can plainly see the difference in the size of the net area that is covered by this move

rather than head and glove first.

Begin this maneuver by throwing your inside leg (the leg that is furthest from the puck) out in the direction in which the puck is travelling. At the same time, kick your outside leg in the same direction, and fling yourself feet first in the direction of the other goalpost. The inside leg, the one that you started this movement with, must lie flat along the ice surface, with the other leg firmly lying on top. You will still be able to reach over with your free arm and cover some more area directly above your pads.

When you practice this maneuver, do it well out from the net so you won't damage your skate blades by striking the far post.

Catching the Puck

I have often seen young goaltenders make one fundamental mistake. When a puck is shot hard and right at their chest, they will either move to one side to allow their glove hand to snare the puck or they will drop to their knees to catch the puck, and in doing so, they leave a large part of the net uncovered.

I have always kept my body between the net and the puck. It doesn't matter that I am unable to catch the puck clean in this manner. It goes back to my baseball days as a catcher. Keep your body in front of the ball at all times. The same applies in the game of hockey. It will not look as neat and clean, but you'll make fewer mistakes if you take the safe route. If the puck hits you square in the chest, it is not going to go in the net. If you fail to snare the puck with your catching glove, it will still drop to your feet and you can smother it with your pads.

If you do catch a puck, keep in mind that the play isn't over until the whistle blows. With the puck safely in your glove, keep your glove hand in front of your body. If there's a scrum in your crease or hard charging forwards, and if your glove enters the net with the puck inside of it, the goal still counts.

Defending the Corner Pass-Out

When the puck is in the control of an opposition player in the corner to your glove side, your stance should be as shown in the photograph below—your seat back in the net with your skate jammed tight to the post. The length of your pad should be against the post and your stick flat on the ice and at an angle so that if the puck is shot at your stick, it will not deflect between your skates and into the net. I like to keep my catcher tight to the outside of the post which helps to keep my entire body anchored to the net. In this position you are vulnerable to being checked or interfered with from your blind side. Your defensemen should be aware of this fact and be prepared to prevent it.

When the puck is in the corner to your stick side, the stance remains the same as described at left, except that in this instance your catcher hand can be extended outwards in order to block a flip shot pass-out. Keep in mind that in either instance, your skates and pads must be kept against the post with all of the pressure that you can bring to bear. As seen in the photograph below, I am using my blocker and the shaft of my stick to anchor myself to the post. Remember that you must try to deflect or interfere with the speed and direction of a pass-out from the corner because there will be an opponent waiting somewhere behind you for that pass.

Mark Messier and Glenn Anderson have perfected a routine that stymies the goaltender who leaves his post too quickly on a wrap-around. Messier will carry the puck to the side of the net and pretend to carry it around the back. Goaltenders will tend to leave their post early to try to beat Messier to the other side. Meanwhile Messier will backpass the puck to Anderson who deftly puts it into an empty net. This play demonstrates that *a goaltender must never leave the short side post until he can no longer see the puck*. You will still be able to reach the other side of the net before the forward can complete the wrap-around.

You've Got To Give Them Something

The dimensions of a standard goal net are four feet high and six feet wide. Since there are very few goaltenders who measure that exact same width and height, you have to realize that it is impossible for you to cover the entire area of open net. The question is, "What do you give them?" The answer basically comes down to style. Your style. It is something that you will unconsciously develop over your career, but here is what I do.

Since I have to give something, I make it my strength. My strength has always been my glove hand, so when a shooter is bearing down on me in the net, he will always see a little more opening on my glove side than anywhere else. I am hoping that he will shoot for it.

The other option is to give away their weakness. You might have seen me give up what appears to be an easy goal through the five hole—the area left between the goaltender's legs when he has them open. I developed that style basically because it is my opinion that the five hole is the hardest target to hit. During my career I have been involved in thousands of practices and I have noticed that every forward and defenseman, when skating in on an empty net, will generally try to pick the corners, and usually try to do it high. Rarely does the coach stress the five hole shot and there are no drills designed to teach it—that is until the Shooter-Tooter arrived.

Since I see most forwards practicing shots to the corners, I learned to take away the corners and give them the five hole. If a player can hit it, then fine. Remember, you can't cover everything. However, in the long run, most will miss the five hole shot and the puck will be harmlessly deflected off my pads and into the corner. It is like the forward who always at practice, practiced shooting the puck at the goalpost. During the game, on two consecutive breakaways, he performed perfectly—he hit the goalpost both times.

HERE'S MY ADVICE FOR FORWARDS READING THIS BOOK:

Shoot low on the stick side. I think most goaltenders will agree that the goalie is weakest there. On this type of shot, when the goaltender moves his stick in the stick-side direction, the toe of the stick will come up off the ice leaving just enough room for the puck to go under. Other than that, shoot for between the legs, the infamous five hole. Most goaltenders will give it to you, so if you can hit the spot, it's yours.

Off-Ice Training

Inner Knee Strengthening

Weightlifting is not too important to the early development of a goaltender. Light weights to develop forearm, wrist and leg muscles are fine, but a goaltender must be agile, not musclebound.

There is one weight training activity, however, that I consider absolutely essential, and *a serious goaltender should be doing this every day.* I have found that the actions performed by a goaltender on the ice build up the outer muscles of the knee. If the inner knee muscles are not developed at the same rate, the knee caps will be gradually pulled to the outside and the result will be knee pain and increasing likelihood of serious injury.

The exercise is simple. It's done sitting down, so you can do it while you read or watch hockey on TV. Attach a light weight to a towel, draping it over the foot and lift the weight by flexing the knee only. A weight of about two pounds is all that is required. Perform this exercise for about ten minutes on each leg per day.

Reflex Drill 1

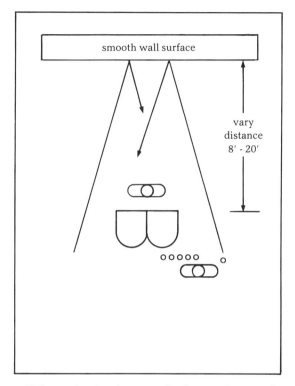

When it is impractical to do goaltender's drills during team practice, you can accomplish some of the same things in a parking lot, in a gymnasium, or in your own basement.

Probably the best off-ice drill for developing reaction skills is the one pictured here. This drill is done against a wall, and requires one helper and five or six tennis balls.

Face the wall at a distance ranging from twelve feet down to about six feet. Have your friend stand behind you, out of your line of sight, and throw the tennis balls at the wall in such a way that they will rebound towards you. Remember that during this drill, you should be using both your catcher and your blocker glove. The object of course, is to catch, block with your body, or your blocking glove the entire number of tennis balls thrown. Have your friend move from side to side, and vary the speed of his throw.

The test becomes much more difficult as you move closer to the wall. Even spending ten minutes a day doing this drill will vastly improve your reaction time. If possible, teaming up with another goalie would be the perfect situation.

I*'ve never seen reflexes like Grant's. I think he's the best goaltender in the history of the NHL.*

• • • • • •

Wayne Gretzky

Reflex Drill 2

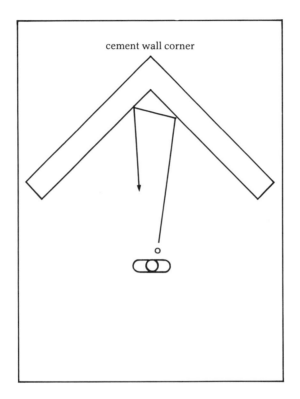

cement wall corner

This is a drill you can do by yourself. Throw a tennis ball into the corner with one hand and catch it with the other. Change hands repeatedly, so you are catching with both weak and strong hands. Vary this drill by hitting the floor with the ball first and then letting it rebound off the wall at you.

You don't really think in hockey, you react all the time.

• • • • • •

Don Cherry

Baseball, Table Tennis, and Video Games

I used to spend my summers on the ball diamond. The equivalent of the goaltender in baseball is the catcher. That's the position I played. It helped develop fast reaction time, and certainly helped my knee and thigh muscles. Bending the knees in that position and jumping to a full stance made a big contribution to my lower body strength. I found, oddly enough, that my goaltending experience also helped my catching in baseball. I learned to block a ball, and I was not afraid of getting hurt. At age 16, I was drafted as a lefty catcher by the Pittsburgh Pirates, but I knew hockey would be my life.

The best indoor off-ice activity related to goaltending is table tennis. It develops hand-eye co-ordination like nothing else. Some computer games and video games are also quite useful. Anything that requires concentration and quick interaction of the hands with the eyes will be helpful.

Grant Fuhr with teammate Mark Messier hamming it up at an Oilers/A.C.T. charity baseball game.

Twelve Tips

1) Keep your body square to the puck at all times.

2) Maintain your concentration.

3) Maintain a cool and even temperament.

4) Spot the puck off to the side of your net for your defensemen.

5) Pads first across the net, not glove first.

6) Keep your stick on the ice at all times.

7) Play the person carrying the puck, not the person you expect to receive the pass.

8) Do inner knee strengthening exercises daily.

9) Return to your net on the same side as you left it.

10) Keep your body between the puck and the net at all times.

11) Play as hard for your team when you are on the bench as when you are on the ice.

12) At all times, have fun.

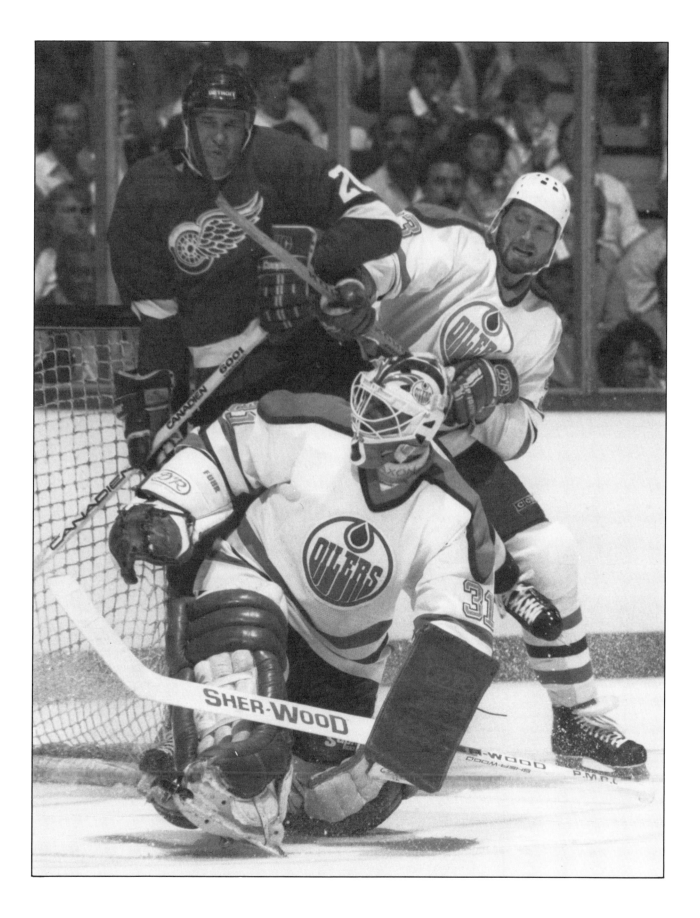

Under pressure, there is
none finer. He proved in the
Canada Cup that he is the
finest goaltender in the
world.

• • • • • •

Ron Low, former Oiler goalie
and current coach of the Cape
Breton Oilers

It's just something that happens. They get frustrated so they run over you. And there you are, out in the middle of the freeway.

• • • • • •

Grant Fuhr, after a bruising playoff game against Detroit in the '88 playoffs.

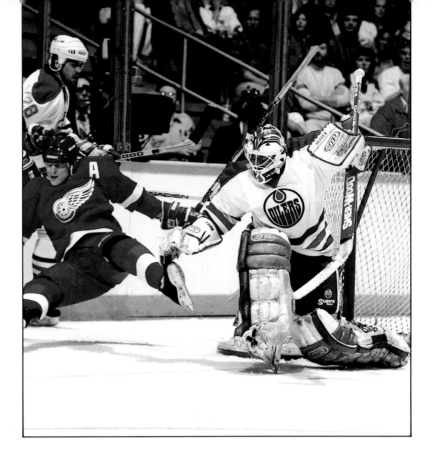

Grant Fuhr is the

Gretzky of the goalies!

• • • • • •

*Detroit Red Wings goalie
Glen Hanlon*

THE GAME

Pre-Game Warm-Up

During the shooting portion of the pre-game warm-up, you must make it a steadfast rule that one player at a time carries the puck in and takes his shot on net. Too often, undisciplined teams, with three minutes to go before the game starts, will begin blasting pucks up around the goaltender's head. If you find yourself in this situation, skate away. Only a fool will stand there and become just a target.

The pre-game warm-up shooting portion is for the goaltender's preparation only. You may have to constantly remind players and coaches of this fact. This part of the warm-up lets the goalie develop a feel for the puck, slowly builds his reaction time to game conditions, and gets him into a good mental frame for the game.

If your teammates, during this phase of the warm-up, are constantly picking corners or blasting the puck into open areas of the net, it can only hurt your team's chances of winning the game. Destroying the confidence of the goaltender before the game starts is not only stupid on the part of the players, but shows a distinct lack of understanding on the part of the coaches.

In the pre-game activity, players should be directing soft shots at the goaltender. As the goaltender begins to warm up, the strength of the shots should be slowly increased until they reach full potential, just at the conclusion of the warm-up.

Preparing the Crease

You have often seen a goaltender, at the start of the game, enter the area of his net and skate back and forth in his crease, using a scraping motion with his skates. This preparation of the crease before the beginning of play is very important. This area of ice must be smoothed after each new flooding.

If you watch the ice being flooded, you'll notice that the Zamboni passes over the crease area at both ends of the ice at least six or seven times while it passes over the rest of the ice surface only once. This eventually builds up a mound or hill in the crease, as well as forming waves by the water build-up. The side to side scraping will even this out substantially and you will avoid the possibility of tripping during a side to side movement. Also, and just as important, smoothing out this area will eliminate the possibility that the puck will hit a bump or mound and skip up and over your goalstick.

During the game, it is also important to minimize the build-up of snow in your crease area. Whether you sweep it to the side of your net or into your net really makes no difference.

Temperament

The goaltender in the junior leagues as well as the NHL is becoming more and more of a target. With opposition players assigned to block the net or screen the goalie and harrass him, temperament has become a big factor in a goaltender's makeup.

I have never had much of a temper and have always been able to ignore most of what goes on in my immediate area. The goaltenders who don't ignore this facet of the game as much as possible can really hurt their team with their retaliation penalties. You must have faith in the referees, and bring any undue infractions incurred upon you to their attention.

Generally some rough stuff involving myself and a player from the other team will only strengthen my resolve to play better. That is the only way a goaltender can in the end get even—by letting fewer goals in than your opponent at the opposite end.

When a goaltender lets it be known that the opposition's behavior is bothering him and is getting him off his game, he is playing into the hands of the other team. Be cool and remain calm and let them see a minimum of your emotions. Develop a very patient and cool temperament. In the long run this will become one of your most useful weapons.

You must also remember that you are out there alone. When you make a mistake, it is seen by all. Others make mistakes that are masked or hidden, but when you make one, that little red light points out the fact for all to see. I have found it best to shut out both the cheers and the jeers. A carefree attitude must be put on at the same time as you strap on the pads.

I wish I could be more like Grant. The more pressure there is, the calmer he gets.

• • • • • •

Corinne Fuhr, Grant's wife

76

I *don't get mad. I don't*

worry. There's no sense in it.

• • • • • •

Grant Fuhr

Communication

Part of the goaltender's job is to be the eyes of his defensemen. A good part of the time that the puck is in your end, it is behind the goal line. This means that the defensemen are facing towards you, and facing away from the attacking zone. In this situation, the goaltender must let his defensemen know what the opposition players are doing.

Nowadays, with offensive defensemen, the defenseman from either point will pinch in toward the net when the puck is behind the goal line. This has proven to be a very successful play because most of your teammates will be facing the puck or at least looking in its direction. You must always be aware of what is happening and let your teammates know.

Communication is also important when one of your teammates is carrying the puck around the back of your net. He must be kept informed if there is a man on him or if someone is cutting across the front of the net to cut him off. If one of your wingers is open, his location will be useful information for your teammate to have. It will be easier for everyone if you tell him the area that is open rather than name the player that is open. Communication is a key when the puck is in your end. Keep up the chatter.

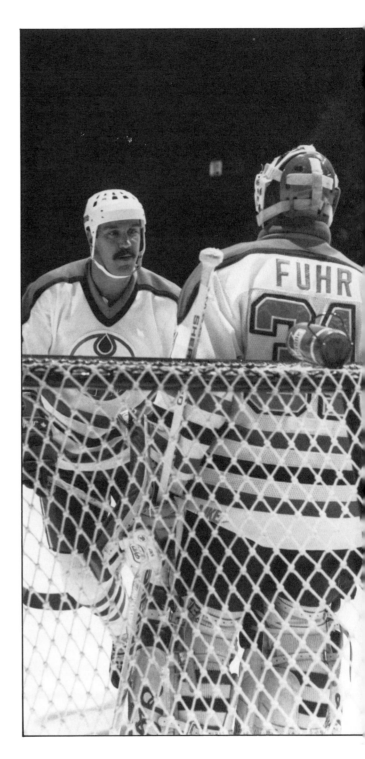

The Faceoff

Remember that placing players in position for faceoffs in your end is not your job. It is the coach's job. The only time that I make an exception to that rule is when one of my players is blocking my view of an important area of the ice. Then and only then will I ask the player to move.

Before the puck is dropped, I will scan the ice and determine where all of the opponent's players are. Knowing where everybody is will help you to guess where the puck is going if their centerman wins the faceoff. Every team has set patterns that they follow in the event that they win the faceoff. It is always a practiced play, so after you have played the team a couple of times, you should know what to expect.

Once I have scanned the ice and determined where their players are, it is then a matter of establishing my position.

I will come out to the top corner of my crease, make sure that I am centered on my net, and then watch the puck. Keep a sharp eye out for the player who likes to one-time the puck at the net right off the faceoff. When Garry Unger was playing for the Oilers, he spent a few minutes after a practice one day showing Wayne Gretzky how to slap the puck out of the air at the net on the faceoff. That night we were playing St. Louis and Wayne pulled this trick on Mike Luit. I have seen him do it a couple of times since and I still am amazed. Now that he is playing for Los Angeles, I will have to be ready to face that one myself a few times.

Usually, however, if the opposition centerman wins the faceoff, he will try to get the puck to either of their point men who will try to get the puck on the net as quickly as possible, while their forwards charge the net looking for the rebound.

Playing the Two On One

Two opposition players are carrying the puck into your zone, and you have only one defenseman defending. The steadfast rule applies: *the goaltender must take or play the puck-carrier, and the defenseman must defend against the pass.* The defenseman must stay between the puck-carrier and his open teammate, in a position to intercept any pass that might be attempted. He in effect takes the second forward out of the play, leaving it as a one on one against the goaltender. If the defenseman stays in the slot area in front of the net while he is backing in, this also takes away the possibility of the puck-carrier cutting across the net, and thus getting the goalie out of position.

When the play has been effectively reduced to a one on one, the goaltender must come out of his net, no more than a foot or two beyond the crease, and cut down the angle. If the puck-carrier is coming in off to one side of the ice, I will cheat a little and take away the center of the net, trying to force him to go to the short side. Doing this offers him a much smaller area to shoot at, and if you are quick enough, it will usually offer him no option other than to shoot right at you.

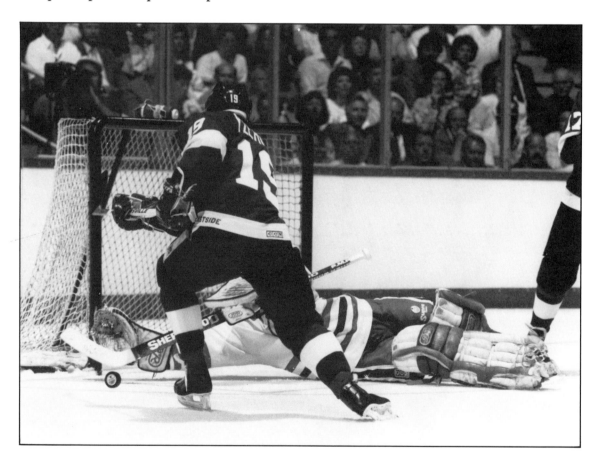

Playing the Breakaway

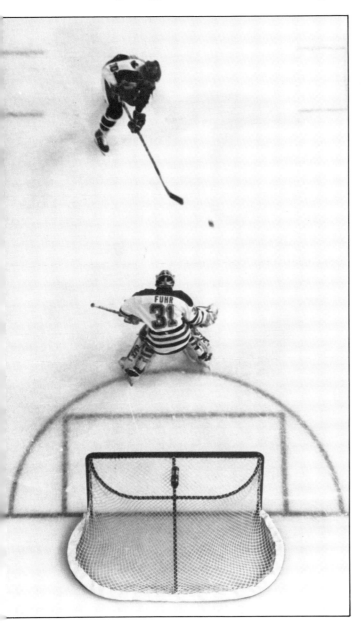

The breakaway. One of the most horrifying moments for the goaltender. Within seconds you will feel like a hero or a bum. You must keep in mind that on a breakaway the goaltender has the odds in his favor. It is tough to keep up your confidence during the breakaway, but it is a must.

First, you must come out of your net to meet the shooter. This cuts down the angle. Sometimes I will give the shooter an opening to the glove side early in hopes that he will shoot from well out, but usually he will elect to move in.

As the shooter approaches you, start your movement back into the net. Keep your weight on the flat of the blades of your skates as this will allow you to move to either side faster. Remember that most players on a breakaway will tend to go to their backhand. Determine in your mind early whether he is right- or left-handed and which side of your net will be his backhand side.

The next thing you must do is nothing. Just by standing there, you will force the shooter to make the first move. If he makes the first move, he is at your mercy. It takes nerves of steel, and most times you feel you are making a mistake by not anticipating his move and going first, but if you go first, the puck will be in the net. *You must force the shooter to make the first move.*

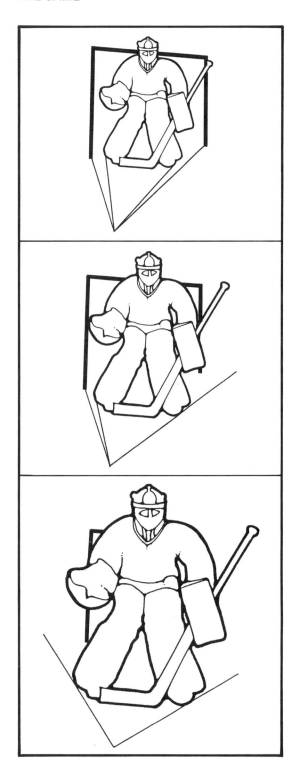

Playing the Angles

The accompanying illustrations easily show the effect that cutting down the angles has in decreasing the area of the net available to an attacking forward. Coming out of your net to meet the shooter, pausing slightly, and then backing in towards your net as he approaches is all a matter of timing which is developed in practice.

If the puck carrier starts to move across to the other side of the net, you must move with him, keeping yourself between him and the net. Remember that it is the puck that must enter the net and not the player shooting it. Keep your concentration on the puck and not the player's body.

Forward Passing

Watching the Oilers, you may have noticed that when the opposition has dumped the puck into our zone, I will often cut the puck off behind the net and shoot it up to one of our waiting forwards just inside the red line, thus executing a very fast and often very successful break-

out. This play is not generally recommended when your team is on a power-play.

When we are on a powerplay and the opposition has legally iced the puck, I will either stop the puck behind the net and set it up for one of my defensemen, or I will let it go around to where he can pick it up just inside our blue line, take it behind our net, and set up another line rush.

At even strength, oftentimes the other team will dump the puck in for a line change. Then, if I see an opening, a forward will hold at the red line and I make the pass. In this way, the Oilers keep getting the three on ones and four on twos that they seem to get more than other teams. Try this at practice. Remember that your forward receiving the pass must have at least one foot on your side of the red line or the play will be called as a two-line or offside pass. Also remember that this play should only be used when the teams are at even strength and the opposition team can be caught taking their line change.

When our team has a five on three advantage and there is a faceoff in the opposition's end, you will notice that I take up a position in the slot, sometimes almost to my blue line. This is designed so that if the opposition gets possession of the puck and ices it, I am able to cut off the icing much earlier, gain control of the puck and forward pass it to one of our players. This basically cuts the ice in half and helps our team keep up a sustained attack for the length of the two-man advantage.

Asleep at the Switch

Believe me, it's easy to do. You are in the nets for forty or forty-five minutes. The opposition has had only one or two shots on your net in the last ten minutes, and you "fall asleep." It has happened to everyone who has ever played goal. I have found that the best defense is to be aware that it will happen. During periods of slow play in my end, I fight to maintain my concentration. Staying alert and intent on the position of the puck at all times does help.

During stoppages in play, you'll notice many goaltenders will skate out of their nets and skate to one corner in their end and back. I have made it a habit to skate to our bench whenever there is a penalty called on the opposition. Doing this type of thing keeps you in the game. Go to the bench, have a sip of water and a few words with the coach or the players, and back into the nets. Just the change of pace helps.

The 100-foot floater that skips on the ice just before reaching you and flips over your glove or stick into the net happens to all of us at one time or another. When it does happen, ignore it as best you can and go on. Be aware that it can happen at any time. Be alert, concentrate on the puck, and stay in the game.

The Hook

The goaltender's nightmare. Being relieved of duty during the game can be an emotional strain. Remember at all times that this is a coaching decision and not one that you should ever make yourself. Keep in mind as well that goaltending changes come about quite often as an attempt to shock the team into action, and not solely because of the goaltender's play.

When it does happen, go to the bench quickly and quietly. Cheer on your teammates, be positive on the bench. A goaltender that conducts himself in this manner under these trying conditions will always attract the attention of both the scouts and his coaches, and will be appreciated as a team player.

Remember, too, that it takes at least two mistakes to allow a goal. One of those two mistakes is always made by you. Shoulder your part of the responsibility, and resolve to not let that particular situation lead to a goal again. The mistakes made by your defensemen or forwards are not your concern. They may be something that can be talked through later at practice, but it is a bad policy to cast blame during the game. Remember, in all situations where a goal is scored on you, at least half of the blame lies on your shoulders. Carry it honorably and turn each one into a positive learning experience.

Scouting the Opposition's Goaltender

When you are in the nets, your job is to stop the puck. If some scouting of the opposition goaltender is needed, then it is the job of the backup goaltender to perform this duty. It is often very helpful for your team to receive a mini scouting report on the other goalie between periods. The backup goaltender is in the best position in the house to do this job. It also helps to keep him in the game while putting in the two and a half hours on the bench. It is always helpful to know whether the opposition goalie goes down too quick, or not at all, or is weak stacking his pads and instead dives head first across the net. Identifying these weaknesses should always be the job of the backup netminder.

EQUIPMENT

There is no doubt about it—outfitting a goaltender in all of the finest equipment available is a very expensive process. Luckily, at the minor hockey levels, most of the more expensive items are usually supplied. Using this equipment is certainly recommended at least until you are at the late stages of bantam or midget levels. Once you have reached the midget level and if you are determined that goaltending is something that you are adept at and are interested in pursuing further, then it's time to look into purchasing your own personally-fitted equipment. Quite often in minor hockey the equipment is purchased with the average-sized goal-tender in mind. If you are in excess of the average in weight or height, or below the same averages, you may find yourself in a bit of a problem as far as proper fit is concerned.

Wearing oversized equipment will offer you more protection, but it will also be more bulky and heavier and thus will slow your reaction times down. On the other hand, equipment that is too small will be lighter and may allow you to move a little quicker, but it won't offer you total protection in all areas. This may not be too much of a problem, however, until you reach the levels of senior bantam and midget.

Skates

Goaltenders skates differ from the skates used by the rest of the players in many ways. If you are going to play goal on a regular basis, proper goal skates are a must. They offer much heavier protection in the boot, as well as having the heavy plastic covering on the inside or instep area. The blades are built of heavier metal and the uprights between the blades and boot are much sturdier and will normally take the heavy hit from a puck. The sole of the boot is built so that it is closer to the ice than in normal skates.

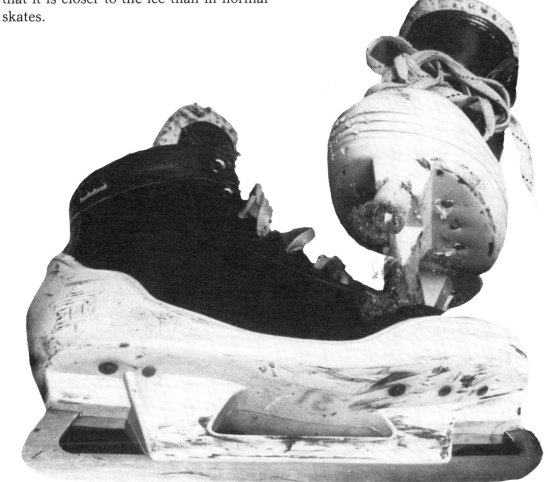

Skate Sharpening

For a forward or a defenseman, speed is of the essence, and it has been found that a rockered blade presents less blade surface to the ice and therefore less friction and hence greater speed. The goaltender relies much less on skate speed and much much more on standing balance. Therefore, it is important for the goaltender's skates to be flatter over the length of the blade. In this way, the skate presents a longer blade area within which to maintain balance.

There is a process which is used everywhere now of hollowing the blades of forwards' skates—putting in a slight groove down the length of the blade. This presents two sharp edges and a resessed center which allows the player to cut very sharp corners. However, this treatment would restrict the side to side motion needed by the goaltender. The goaltender's skates should be sharpened relatively flat and should be slightly dulled immediately after each sharpening. That way, the goaltender can slide his skates sideways without the blade grabbing on the ice surface. The more blade contacting the ice surface, the better for maintaining balance.

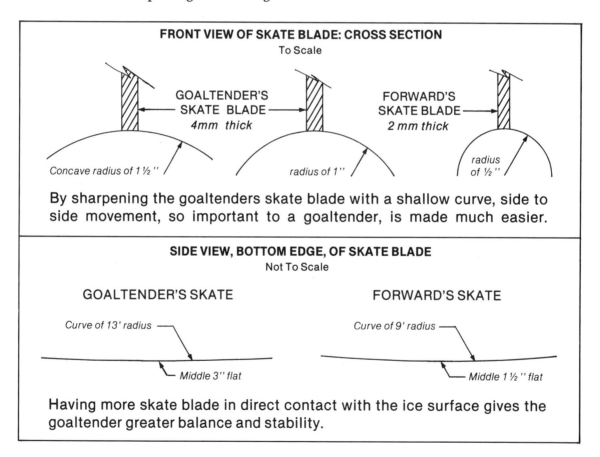

FRONT VIEW OF SKATE BLADE: CROSS SECTION
To Scale

GOALTENDER'S SKATE BLADE
4mm thick

FORWARD'S SKATE BLADE
2 mm thick

Concave radius of 1 ½ ''

radius of 1''

radius of ½ ''

By sharpening the goaltenders skate blade with a shallow curve, side to side movement, so important to a goaltender, is made much easier.

SIDE VIEW, BOTTOM EDGE, OF SKATE BLADE
Not To Scale

GOALTENDER'S SKATE

FORWARD'S SKATE

Curve of 13' radius

Curve of 9' radius

Middle 3'' flat

Middle 1 ½ '' flat

Having more skate blade in direct contact with the ice surface gives the goaltender greater balance and stability.

Goalie Pants

Don't be fooled. There is a big difference between the pants worn by your forwards and the pants that you should be wearing. Pants made especially for goaltenders have much more generous padding on the thigh front portion, as well as padding on the inside of the thighs. This may not be too important at the lower levels of hockey, but by the time you have reached bantam and midget levels, this extra bit of protection becomes a necessity.

Be certain there is no gap between your pads and your pants. The top of your pads should extend over the bottom of the goalie's pants by at least two inches when standing erect.

Pads

Pads are a goaltender's best friend. They will do more to protect you than any other piece of equipment. And of course, the bigger the pads, the more area of the net they will cover. The only drawback, in the past anyway, has been that bigger meant heavier. A pair of goalie pads will increase in weight almost 50 percent during the course of a game due to the absorption of water. However with the new style of pads now coming onto the market, the absorption factor is being reduced all the time, as well as the general overall weight.

I have always preferred my pads to come to about the middle of my thigh.

For me, this means a 35½ inch pad.

A little tip on maintaining your pads: rub them with wax occasionally to hold down the water absorption. Also, since the width of pads is a steadfast rule in most hockey leagues, if you find your old pads are widening a touch over the limit, wrap them tightly with hockey tape when they are soaking wet after a game or practice. This will restore their shape for a short time, at least. Also, have them repaired and resewn as soon as a skate cut happens. It is a very inexpensive procedure if it is taken care of right away.

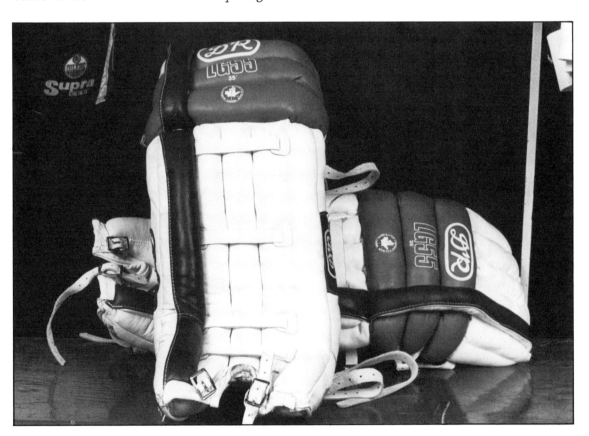

Keep in mind that your goalie pads will not save you from every shot from every angle. It is generally recommended that you wear some sort of knee pad underneath your regular pads. Older pads that do not have the inside leg protection either sewn on or strapped on should be reworked to include these. It's an inexpensive addition, and without it the insides of your knees are left totally unprotected. Minor Hockey associations should be made aware of this problem because a good rap with a puck on the inside of the knee can cause permanent knee damage.

During the 1987-88 season, I tried the new line of lightweight pads. Not being used to such lightweight pads, I found myself moving past the puck. They increased my speed so much that I was actually ahead of the puck when I had never been before. I had to go back to the old pads, and wear the new ones through a full training camp before I was comfortable with the new style.

Newer models that come preformed at the knees and ankles, don't need to be broken in or shaped. Straight pads need to be softened by placing them in a formed position with the knees and ankles bent and keeping them in that position for a period of time. If you can tie them in that position and apply either some steam or heat, it will speed up the process somewhat.

The New Modular Pads

Photo courtesy of Daignault-Rolland

The new modular pads are a completely different type of goal pad. Made of a combination of nylon, plastic, and foam, they are approximately half the weight of traditional leather pads. While leather pads absorb water during a game and become significantly heavier, this new material is designed to repel water, so the weight gain during a game will be lessened. As well, the outer foam shield is claimed to deaden the impact of the puck, allowing the goaltender better control over rebounds.

Neck Protector

Only recently has the neck protector been developed to such an extent that it can be worn as a regular piece of equipment all the time. I tried many of the older models in earlier years and they proved to be just too uncomfortable. With recent developments using materials such as ballistic nylon and softer plastics, I now find that I won't go on the ice without one. A neck protector is designed not only to lessen the blow of a stick or puck striking the front of the neck area, but also to greatly reduce the possibility of skate cuts to this most vulnerable area of the body. Whether or not the goaltender's neck protector is mandatory in your minor hockey association, *wear one.* The goaltender's crease, over the past few years, has seen more and more close-in action. When a goaltender is down and there is a crowd in the crease, the goaltender's virtually at the mercy of the protective equipment he has on at the time. Wear a neck protector at all times.

Catcher

The catcher that I use is as big as the rules allow. Again, with the recent advent of super-lightweight material, my most recent glove is about half the weight of the glove I wore just a few years ago. Some goaltenders prefer to wear a golf glove under their catchers mitt. I never have. I like to feel the sting of the puck hitting the palm of my hand. Then I know I have got it. The use of the golf glove will lessen the sting, and help to keep the glove dry. Some goalies have a separate golf glove to wear each period.

The quickest way to break in a new catcher is to put a little oil on the palm of the glove, tie it up in a closed position and put it into a plastic bag. Using a hair dryer, blow some hot air into the bag and then seal the bag and leave it over-night. By the next day it will be softened enough so that you will be able to work with it. The best way, however, to break in new equipment is to use it. It is going to be stiff and awkward, but unless you can afford two sets of equipment, there is not much else you can do that won't permanently damage or misshape a new piece of equipment.

Blocker

The blocker glove should be kept in good repair as this is the glove that is most often nearest to the ice surface, and the action of sharp skates and the like. Some of the newer blockers have an upturned lip at the top that helps control rebounds. I've found this to be very useful. You have to use every advantage that the rules will allow you.

Mask

On November 1, 1959, Jacques Plante went to the Canadien's dressing room after being hit by a shot, and returned wearing a mask, and so began a new era. Never again would it be considered sissy or cowardly for a goaltender to be seen wearing face protection. Had some of the mystique of the goalie disappeared? Possibly so, but with the curved stick becoming more and more common, it was now impossible to determine exactly where the puck might end up, and the goalie's face became more vulnerable.

During minor hockey years, the helmet with the face cage is of course mandatory. It is always a good idea, however, to add something below the mask to offer neck and collarbone protection. Various types of plastic shields are offered for this use.

During my career, I have used every type of facial protection offered, including some I constructed myself. I have found

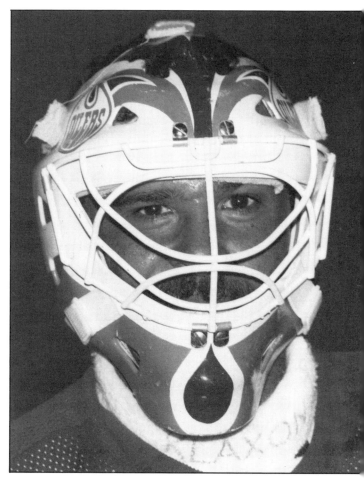

that the solid plastic shield is too hot, and worse, it fogs up. The standard helmet and face cage is good.However, with NHL-type shooting now more common at the junior levels, it simply doesn't offer enough protection. On heavy impact the helmet splits and the edges of the plastic can cause very nasty cuts. I have found that the solid fiber-glass mask offers the best sight lines of all, but it too builds up a tremendous amount of heat. I finally settled on the partial fiberglass mask with the partial cage. The heat dissipation is best, while the fiberglass distributes the blow evenly over a large area, causing bruising and occasionally a goose egg, but I have never received a cut. Over the last few years this mask has become by far the most popular amongst the NHL goaltenders. Keep in mind that a neck protector is still a must.

Goalstick

In choosing a goalstick, the first and most important factor to consider is the lie. The proper lie for you is determined by both your height and your stance. The shorter you are or the more crouch that you use, the lower numbered lie you will need.

Basically, lie numbers start at 12 and in most cases progress in half numbers up to 15. A number 15 is suitable for only the tallest goaltenders. At my height, 5′ 11′′, the lie that I like best is number 14 or 14½. To determine the proper lie for yourself, assume your normal crouch position with the stick in your hand and the blade on the ice. If the blade lies flat along the ice, then that is the proper lie stick. If either the heel of the stick or the toe is raised above the ice surface, then another lie stick would be more suitable. Remember that if you are doing this in a sports shop, not wearing skates, your height is reduced by about 1½ inches. If you find that your current stick is the improper lie for you, you can sometimes compensate for it by shaving the heel down.

My personal stance is considered upright. To enable me to be comfortable, I prefer to use the maximum height allowed on the paddle portion of the stick. Thus when leaning on the stick, I am able to remain fairly erect in my stance. A shorter stick would mean a greater crouch and hinder fast movement within the crease. Check the paddle height on your stick by keeping your blocker hand all the way down the stick. This is where your hand should be at all times. If you find it is not the most comfortable position for you, select a stick with a different paddle height.

I prefer a blade that is slightly curved. I have found that it doesn't affect the rebound direction, but it enables me to handle the puck much more effectively. As well it gives your shot the same extra snap as a forward or defenseman's stick.

Keep in mind when taping your stick that you should never use black or dark-colored tape on the knob end. During a scramble in the crease, a knob with dark tape on it can be mistaken for the puck, and it has been called a goal in this situation when the end of your stick enters the net for even a split second.

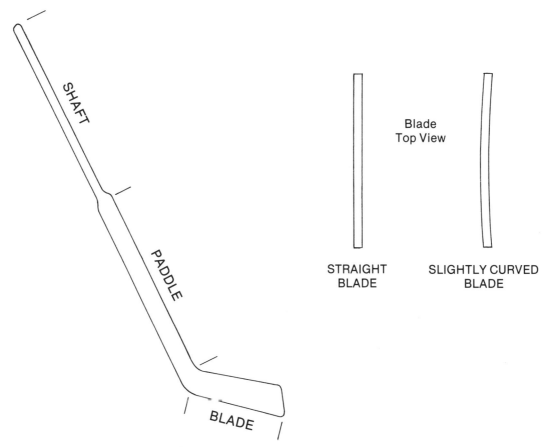

SHAFT

PADDLE

BLADE

Blade
Top View

STRAIGHT
BLADE

SLIGHTLY CURVED
BLADE

Taping the Stick

SCOUTING
WITH BARRY FRASER:
AN INSIDE LOOK

Scouting Grant Fuhr

Barry Fraser is Chief Scout and Director of Player Personnel for the Edmonton Oilers. He first scouted Grant Fuhr in 1980, and is widely recognized as the chief architect of the Oilers success.

There is no doubt in my mind that Grant Fuhr is the best goaltender in the National Hockey League, not only today, but since he first entered the league in 1980. I can't even restrict that statement to just the NHL. In my opinion, he's the best in the world. There just doesn't seem to be any goaltender anywhere in the world today that you can compare with him, unless you go back to Sawchuck and Plante. In my lifetime I have never seen another goaltender as quick to react to the puck as Fuhr.

Grant's style dictates that he plays on his knees a lot, so if he has a weakness, you might say it's low shots right at him. He gives up more goals through the five hole than most goalies, but as he says himself, you have to give up something. Because he gives up the five hole, he's almost impossible to beat on either side.

His greatest assets are his quickness, and more importantly, his ability to stay square to the puck at all times. Rarely do you see him addressing the shooter turned to the side.

The Oilers began to seriously scout Grant during the 1980 - 81 season, which was his last year with Victoria. I saw him play fifteen games that season, and the rest of the scouting staff attended at least forty games that he played in. He had come to our attention the season before. The year we drafted Grant was the same year our other goaltender at that time, Andy Moog, had had a spectacular play-off series defeating the Montreal Canadiens in three games and taking the New York Islanders to six games before losing, so there was some speculation as to whether we should draft a goaltender that year at all. However, our scouting staff insisted that Fuhr be the player we drafted. In fact, we had him ranked as the number one hockey player in the entire country for that year.

As it was, our draft pick that year was the number eighth overall, but had we drafted number one, we still would have taken Fuhr. We were actually amazed that he was still available when our turn came. It doesn't happen very often that goaltenders are drafted in the first round. I don't agree with that and I never will. It's like baseball—if you don't have good pitching, you go nowhere. Drafted, in order, that year was Dale Hawerchuk, Doug Smith, Bobby Carpenter, Ron Francis, Joe Cirella, Jim Benning and

Mark Hunter, and then Grant Fuhr.

As we all know, he had a spectacular first season with the Oilers. He lost his first game of the season playing against Winnipeg, and he then went through to Christmas before he lost another one. Just a phenomenal season for a rookie goaltender. After hurting his shoulder near the end of that first season and having an inactive summer, he came to training camp the next season in fairly poor condition. The coaching staff sent him to the farm team which at that time was located in Moncton, Nova Scotia. With the rather hectic schedule of games that he played there, it didn't take him very long to get back into playing condition and return to the Oilers. He's been one of the major keys to the success of this hockey club ever since.

The Five Hole

Scouting the Goaltender

Basically, the scouting process begins when a player reaches the junior ranks. If we were to scout major midget or major bantam teams, we would need a scouting staff of four hundred people. It just isn't economically feasible. As well, if a player is serious enough about the game and wants to make a career of it, he'll make it to the junior or college ranks. Major junior teams, and often tier two juniors, are scouted regularly.

When I go out to scout a goaltending prospect, I judge him the same way I do a forward or defenseman. Pure hockey talent. As a matter of fact with the scores in many junior games being up in the 8 - 6 or higher range, we don't pay a whole lot of attention to the statistics. For example, the year we drafted Mark Messier, he had only scored one goal, but that didn't have any bearing on our decision at all. Our job is to evaluate talent and bring the best possible talent here.

As far as evaluating a goaltender, his goals against average is generally disregarded. His save percentage statistic is sometimes useful. That's the percentage of saves versus the number of shots taken at him.

The goaltender has to be the toughest position to scout, because you have to see a goaltender play a lot more than you do a skater. I can go out and watch a really good forward and know enough about him in a period and a half so that I don't have to see him play again. That's because all the technical things he can do, he can show you in seven or eight shifts. But a goaltender can stand down there

forever without seeing much action. His team might be very poor, he might be shell shocked, he might be worn out playing game in and game out. He might be tired and therefore going down a lot. You can't make an informed decision regarding a goaltender by just seeing a couple of games. You have to see him a lot more times to get that feeling you must have before you can make a scouting decision. Our general rule of thumb for the Oilers scouting staff is to see a goaltender in at least ten games before an evaluation is made.

On our evaluation form for the Oilers scouting staff, we rate goaltenders on these things:

☐ **USE OF STICK**
— Stick
— Passes from behind net
— Passes through the crease

☐ **CONTROL OF REBOUNDS**
— Deflects shots to corners
— Covers up

☐ **STAND UP**

☐ **ANGLE**

☐ **USE OF HANDS**
— Catching
— Blocker

☐ **DURABILITY**
— Injury
— Protects crease

☐ **SHOTS**
— High
— Low
— Long
— Close

After evaluating and scoring them on those areas, we make a general evaluation. The highest ranking we give is a nine, a "cinch NHL."

You often hear the criticism that a goaltender goes down too much. There's a major distinction between the goaltender who goes down and has trouble getting up, and the goaltender who goes down the same number of times but can regain his feet with balance very quickly.

Grant Fuhr is a butterfly-style goaltender. You'll see him down in the butterfly position, perhaps more than otherNHL goaltenders, but Grant can spring back up to his feet without the help of his arms or stick. He has the strength and quickness in his legs to be able to do this faster than anyone else I've ever seen. This probably has more to do with Grant's success than anything else. Superior leg strength and quickness. When he goes down to block a shot, Fuhr always makes his commitment to the shot, and not to the fake by the forward. He has a good ability to read what the forward is going to do.

As far as age of goaltending prospects, we do look at some in the sixteen age bracket, simply because they might be playing at the junior level, but generally

The Butterfly

seventeen years old is when we start watching them.

Overall size or height of a goaltending prospect is of some importance. However, the NHL offers both ends of the spectrum—a player the size of Ron Hextall at one end, and at the other, Darren Pang of the Chicago Blackhawks, who is probably the smallest goaltender ever to play in the NHL. Obviously, the larger goaltender not only covers more area of the net, but height helps him see over the crease action, and being able to have that overall view is a big help. Larger goaltenders are probably that much more durable, too. But then, a smaller goalie is sometimes quicker, so you have to balance everything out.

A lot more emphasis is being put on the puck-handling ability of young goaltenders. A goaltender today has to be able to stop those wrap-arounds at the back of the net and then be able to put the puck back into play. If he can do that, he's the sixth man in his own team's zone while the other team has only got five. It is important that he be able to use a lot of outlets to get his team out of trouble in their own end. He must be able to handle the puck effectively and shoot it up along the boards, completing forward passes and so forth. A big part of the change from defense to offense, particularly in the defensive zone, now depends on that ability in your goaltender.

We also like to see a goaltender who can shoot the puck from his natural side, who can stop the puck and shoot it without changing hands on the stick. However, there have been some awfully good goaltenders that haven't been able to do that, but most of those types of

goalies have other puck-handling problems. It's a difficult thing for goaltenders to master, but it's becoming increasingly important from the scouting aspect. It's well worth the time and effort it takes to master shooting and stopping the puck without changing hands if a young goaltender aspires to the NHL these days. That aspect alone increases the goaltender's worth and ability by about ten or fifteen percent.

I'm often asked what the chances are of a young person making it into the NHL ranks. When you take all of the registered minor hockey players in Canada, only one percent end up in the league. Then when you take into account the fact that there are really only two goaltending positions on each NHL team, obviously the odds of becoming employed full time as a goaltender in the NHL are fairly remote. This is why you always hear education being stressed as the most important thing for aspiring goaltenders or any players for that matter.

I'm also asked whether it's better to take the college route to the NHL or go through the major junior ranks. Obviously, if a player is academically inclined, the college route is preferred. However, the junior leagues offer a more lengthy schedule of games and a far more rigorous training regimen. The largest percentage of NHL players come through the junior ranks, but in the last few years more and more players have been coming out of the U.S. college circuit. It really is a decision that must be left up to the individual and the family involved. It's obviously a decision of major importance, and at all times the educational aspect must be considered.

C.A.H.A.
RULES and REGULATIONS

Canadian Amateur Hockey Assocation

The following excerpts are taken from the C.A.H.A. Official Hockey Rules, 1986-1987.

Goal Posts and Nets

Rule 4.

a) In the center of the goal lines between the side boards, regulation goal posts and nets of approved design and materials, shall be placed in such a manner as to remain stationary during the game. It is recommended that the posts on which the nets are placed, do not protrude more than 2 in. (5.08 cm) above the ice surface.

b) The goal posts shall be set 6 ft. (1.83 m) apart, measured from the inside of the posts. They shall extend 4 ft. (1.22 m) vertically from ice surface and a cross bar of the same material as the goal posts shall be extended horizontally from the top of the other posts. The cross bar should be securely fastened to both goal posts. The outside measurement of both the goal posts and the cross bar shall be 2 in. (5.08 cm) in diameter. The area enclosed by the goal posts and the cross bar shall be known as "the Goal".

c) A net of approved design and material shall be attached to the back of each goal.

(Note): *To reduce the possibility of a puck passing through the net and coming out without being detected as a goal, the Rules Committee recommends that each club check the size of the mesh and strength of the cordage. Drape nets are permissible inside the main net. The Art Ross net may be used for C.A.H.A. games.*

d) **NEW** The goal posts, cross bar and the exterior surface of other supporting framework for the goal shall be painted red. The surface of the base plate inside the goal and supports other than the goal posts shall be painted in a light color.

e) **NEW** Nets restrained by magnetic fastening devices may be utilized in C.A.H.A. games.

Goal Crease

Rule 5.

a) In front of each goal, a "Goal Crease" area shall be marked by a red line 2 in. (5.08 cm) wide.

b) The goal crease shall be laid out as follows: 1 ft. (30.48 cm) from the outside of each goal post, lines 4 ft. (1.22 m) in length and 2 in. (5.08 cm) in width shall be drawn at right angles to the goal line and the points of these lines farthest from the goal line shall be joined by another line 2 in. (5.08 cm) in width.

c) The goal crease area shall include all the space outlined by the crease lines and extending vertically to the level of the top of the goal frame.

Sticks

Rule 21.

c) The goalkeeper's stick shall not exceed 55 inches (1.4 m) from the heel to the end of the shaft. The blade of the goalkeeper's stick shall not exceed 3½ inches (8.89 cm) in width at any point nor be less than 3 inches (7.62 cm), except at the heel where it must not exceed 4½ inches (11.43 cm) in width; the goalkeeper's stick shall not exceed 15½ inches (39.37

cm) in length from the heel to the end of the blade.

The widened portion of the goalkeeper's stick extending up the shaft from the blade shall not exceed 26 inches (66.04 cm) in length, calculated from the heel, and shall not exceed 3½ inches (8.89 cm) nor be less than 3 inches (7.62 cm) in width.

NEW The curvature of the blade of the goalkeeper's stick shall not exceed ½ inch (1.27 cm) and shall be measured in the same manner as a player's stick.

d) A Minor penalty shall be assessed any player, including the goalkeeper, for using a stick which does not conform to the provisions of this rule.

e) A Minor penalty plus a Gross Misconduct penalty shall be assessed any player who deliberately breaks a stick when asked to produce same for a measurement or who refuses to surrender his stick for measurement.

g) The stick may be wound with tape of any color.

Goalkeeper's Equipment

Rule 23.

a) With the exception of skates and stick, all the equipment worn by the goalkeeper must be constructed solely for the purpose of protection of the head or body, and must not include any garment or contrivance which would give the goalkeeper undue assistance in keeping goal.

(Note): *Protective padding attached to the back of, or forming part of, the goalkeeper's blocker glove shall not exceed eight inches (20.3 cm) in width nor sixteen inches (40.6*

cm) in length. The base of the goalkeeper's catching glove shall be restricted to a maximum of nine inches (22.9 cm) in width, which is to include any attachments added to that glove. The length of the catching glove is restricted to a maximum of sixteen inches (40.6 cm). The lacing or webbing or other material joining the thumb and index finger of a goalkeeper's glove, or any cage, pocket or pouch created by this material, must not exceed the minimum amount of material necessary to fill the gap between the thumb and the index finger when they are fully extended and spread.

Abdominal aprons extending down the thighs on the outside of the pants are prohibited.

b) Goalkeepers' pads, when new, shall not exceed ten inches (25.4 cm) in extreme width as measured on the goalkeeper, and shall not be altered in any way. No more than one inch (2.54 cm) of expansion, due to wear, shall be permitted.

c) A Minor penalty shall be assessed a goalkeeper guilty of using or wearing illegal equipment.

d) A goalkeeper shall remove his face protector for purpose of identification, if so asked by the Referee. A goalkeeper who refuses this request shall be assessed a Gross Misconduct penalty.

Protective Equipment

Rule 24.

a) All protective equipment except gloves, head gear or goalkeepers' leg pads must be worn entirely under the uniform....

NEW (Note 2): *Goalkeepers in all divisions of hockey shall be required to wear a CSA* *approved hockey helmet to which a CSA approved facial protector has been securely attached and not altered in any way. It is recommended that all goaltenders wear a throat protector.*

Goalkeeper Penalties

Rule 37.

a) No goalkeeper shall be sent to the penalty bench for an infraction which incurs a Minor, Major or Misconduct penalty. Instead, such a penalty shall be served by any player of his team who was on the ice when the infraction occurred. Such player shall be designated by the Manager or Coach of the penalized team, through the Captain.

b) An alternate goalkeeper may replace a regular goalkeeper who has been assessed a Game Misconduct or a Match penalty. In the event there is no alternate goalkeeper recorded on the playing line-up, the regular goalkeeper's place may be taken by any player on the Game Report designated by the Manager or Coach of the penalized team through the Captain. Such substitute will be allowed fifteen minutes to put on the full goalkeeper's equipment.

c) When a goalkeeper leaves the goal crease during a fight, he shall be assessed a Minor penalty, plus any other penalties he might receive.

d) When a goalkeeper leaves his goal crease to join in a fight, act as a peace-maker, or take part in another fight, during the same stoppage of play, he shall receive a Game Misconduct penalty, plus other penalties he shall incur.

e) **NEW** If a goalkeeper intentionally participates in the play in any manner when he is beyond the center red line, he shall be assessed a Minor penalty.

f) A Minor penalty shall be assessed a goalkeeper who, after catching the puck, drop kicks the puck. If injury results, a Major penalty shall be assessed.

PERSONAL RECORDS

Grant Fuhr in NHL All-Star Games

1981 - 82, along with Edmonton Oiler teammates Paul Coffey, Wayne Gretzky, and Mark Messier.

1983 - 84, along with teammates Glenn Anderson, Paul Coffey, Wayne Gretzky, Jari Kurri, Kevin Lowe, Mark Messier, and coach Glen Sather.

1984 - 85, along with teammates Glenn Anderson, Paul Coffey, Wayne Gretzky, Mike Krushelnyski, Jari Kurri, Kevin Lowe, Andy Moog, and coach Glen Sather.

1985 - 86, along with teammates Glenn Anderson, Paul Coffey, Lee Fogolin, Wayne Gretzky, Jari Kurri, Kevin Lowe, Mark Messier, Andy Moog, and coach Glen Sather.

1986 - 87, along with teammates Glenn Anderson, Paul Coffey, Wayne Gretzky, Jari Kurri, Mark Messier, Esa Tikkanen.

1987 - 88, along with teammates Glenn Anderson, Wayne Gretzky, Jari Kurri, Kevin Lowe, Mark Messier, and coach Glenn Sather.

NHL Records

MOST GAMES, ONE SEASON,
BY A GOALTENDER

75 — Grant Fuhr, 1987-88

MOST ASSISTS, ONE SEASON,
BY A GOALTENDER

14 — Grant Fuhr, 1983-84

MOST WINS BY A GOALTENDER,
ONE PLAYOFF YEAR

16 — Grant Fuhr, 1987-88

MOST PENALTY SHOTS FACED AND STOPPED,
ONE PLAYOFF YEAR AND SERIES

2 — Grant Fuhr, 1984-85, Stanley Cup Final against Philadelphia, May 28 and May 30, 1985

NHL Awards

Vezina Trophy, Outstanding Goaltender, 1987 - 88

Edmonton Oilers, Regular Season Records

MOST GAMES APPEARED IN BY A
GOALTENDER, CAREER

330 — Grant Fuhr, 1981-82 through 87-88

MOST CONSECUTIVE COMPLETE GAMES
BY A GOALTENDER

20 — Grant Fuhr, December 22, 1987
through February 3, 1988

MOST ASSISTS, ONE SEASON, GOALTENDER

14 — Grant Fuhr, 1983-84 (NHL record)

MOST PENALTY MINUTES, ONE SEASON,
GOALTENDER

16 — Andy Moog, 1982-83 and
Grant Fuhr, 1987-88

MOST SHUTOUTS, CAREER

6 — Grant Fuhr in 7 seasons,
330 games played

MOST SHUTOUTS, ONE SEASON

4 — Grant Fuhr, 1987-88

LONGEST UNDEFEATED STREAK BY
A GOALTENDER

23 games — Grant Fuhr, October 21/81
through January 13/82, 15 wins, 8 ties

LONGEST SHUTOUT SEQUENCE BY
A GOALTENDER

124 Minutes, 26 Seconds
— Grant Fuhr shutout Minnesota for final
18:09 on December 6/87, shutout Winnipeg for 60:00 on December 9/87, and
shutout Vancouver for initial 46:17 on
December 11/87

Edmonton Oilers, Playoff Records

MOST GAMES APPEARED IN BY
A GOALTENDER

87 — Grant Fuhr, 1982 through 1988

MOST CONSECUTIVE COMPLETE GAMES
BY A GOALTENDER

44 — Grant Fuhr, April 12/86
through May 26/88

MOST CONSECUTIVE COMPLETE GAMES
BY A GOALTENDER, ONE SEASON

18 — Grant Fuhr, April 6/88
through May 26/88

MOST WINS BY A GOALTENDER,
ONE PLAYOFF YEAR

16 — Grant Fuhr, 1988, in 18 games
(NHL record)

MOST CONSECUTIVE WINS BY
A GOALTENDER, ONE PLAYOFF YEAR

9 — Grant Fuhr, April 10/85
through May 7/85

MOST MINUTES PLAYED BY A GOALTENDER

5092 — Grant Fuhr, 1982 through 1988

MOST MINUTES PLAYED BY A GOALTENDER,
ONE PLAYOFF YEAR

1148 — Grant Fuhr, 1987

MOST PENALTY SHOTS FACED,
ONE PLAYOFF YEAR AND SERIES

2 — Grant Fuhr, 1985 Stanley Cup Final
Series vs Philadelphia, May 28, and
May 30, 1985 (NHL record)

MOST PENALTY SHOTS STOPPED,
ONE PLAYOFF YEAR AND SERIES

2 — Grant Fuhr, 1985 Stanley Cup Final
Series vs Philadelphia, May 28 and
May 30, 1985 (NHL record)

Grant Fuhr, Personal Stats, 1981-82 to 1987-88

Regular Season:
GPI - 330; MINS - 18710; GA - 1148; EN - 17;
SO - 6; GAA - 3.68; RECORD - 188-80-42

Playoffs:
GP - 87; MINS - 5092; GA - 255; EN - 7;
SO - 1; GAA - 3.00; RECORD - 63-21

Victoria Cougars Annual Awards

(Left to right) *Bob Smith, Barry Pederson, Grant Fuhr, Mark Robinson, Brad Palmer*

Grant, at 17, winning Rookie of the Year, Most Popular Player, and Most Valuable Player awards. He won 30 of 43 games in his first year, with 2 shutouts.

Rink Diagrams

We've included some blank rink diagrams on the following pages where you can record your own personal drills. You can photocopy these rink diagram pages if you need additional copies.

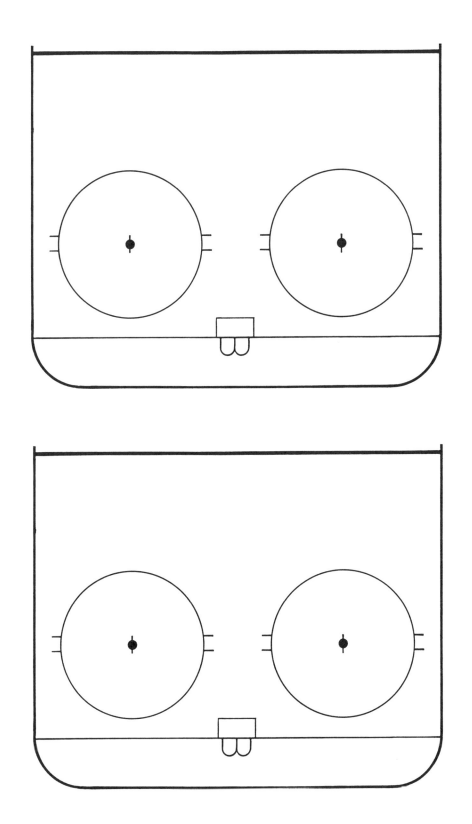

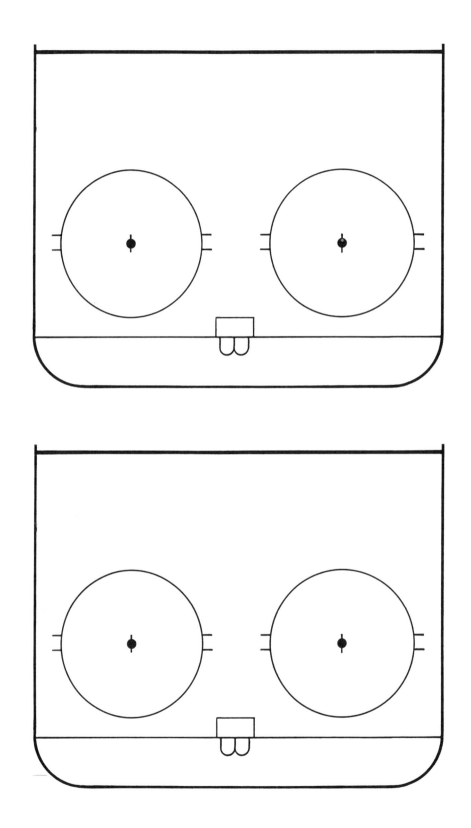

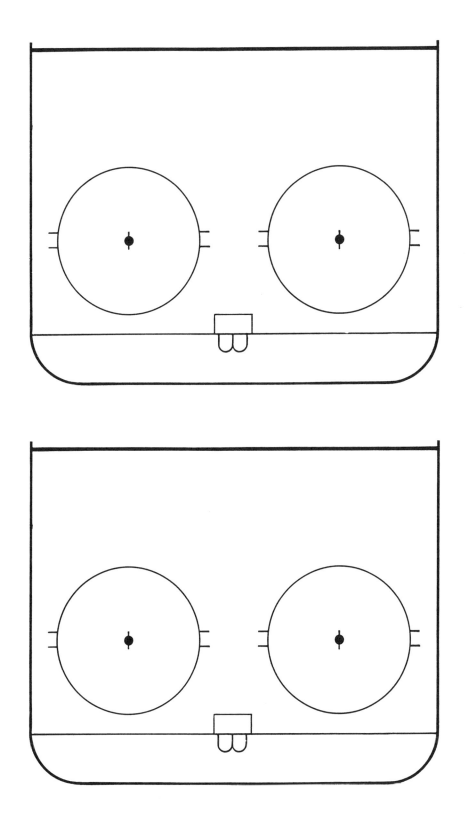